MATH TRAILBLAZERS™

GRADE 2

SECOND EDITION

Student Guide
Book One

A Mathematical Journey Using Science and Language Arts

KENDALL/HUNT PUBLISHING COMPANY
4050 Westmark Drive   Dubuque, Iowa 52002

A TIMS® Curriculum
University of Illinois at Chicago

MATH TRAILBLAZERS™

Dedication

This book is dedicated to
the children and teachers
who let us see the magic
in their classrooms
and to our families who
wholeheartedly
supported us while we
searched for
ways to make it happen.

The TIMS Project

  UIC The University of Illinois at Chicago

The original edition was based on work supported by the National Science Foundation under grant No. MDR 9050226 and the University of Illinois at Chicago. Any opinions, findings, and conclusions or recommendations expressed in this publication are those of the authors and do not necessarily reflect the views of the granting agencies.

Printed in the United States of America

1   2   3   4   5   6   7   8   9   10   07   06   05   04   03

Acknowledgments

Teaching Integrated Mathematics and Science (TIMS) Project Directors

Philip Wagreich, Principal Investigator
Joan L. Bieler
Marty Gartzman
Howard Goldberg (emeritus)
Catherine Randall Kelso

Director, Second Edition

Catherine Randall Kelso

Curriculum Developers, Second Edition

Lindy M. Chambers-Boucher
Elizabeth Colligan
Marty Gartzman
Carol Inzerillo

Catherine Randall Kelso
Jennifer Mundt Leimberer
Georganne E. Marsh
Leona Peters
Philip Wagreich

Editorial and Production Staff, Second Edition

Kathleen R. Anderson
Ai-Ai C. Cojuangco
Andrada Costoiu
Erika Larson
Georganne E. Marsh
Cosmina Menghes
Anne Roby

TIMS Professional Developers

Barbara Crum
Craig Cleve
Elizabeth Colligan
Pamela Guyton

Carol Inzerillo
Linda Miceli
Leona Peters
Jane Schlichting

TIMS Director of Media Services

Henrique Cirne-Lima

TIMS Research Staff

Catherine Randall Kelso
Barry Booton
Dibyen Majumdar

TIMS Administrative Staff

Ora Benton
David Cirillo
Enrique Puente

Principal Investigators, First Edition

Philip Wagreich, Project Director
Howard Goldberg

Acknowledgments

Senior Curriculum Developers, First Edition

Joan L. Bieler
Janet Simpson Beissinger
Astrida Cirulis
Marty Gartzman
Howard Goldberg

Carol Inzerillo
Andy Isaacs
Catherine Randall Kelso
Leona Peters
Philip Wagreich

Curriculum Developers, First Edition

Janice C. Banasiak
Lynne Beauprez
Andy Carter
Lindy M. Chambers-Boucher
Kathryn Chval
Diane Czerwinski

Jenny Knight
Sandy Niemiera
Janice Ozima
Polly Tangora
Paul Trafton

Illustrator, First Edition

Kris Dresen

Research Consultant, First Edition

Andy Isaacs

Mathematics Education Consultant, First Edition

Paul Trafton

National Advisory Committee, First Edition

Carl Berger
Tom Berger
Hugh Burkhardt
Donald Chambers
Naomi Fisher
Glenda Lappan

Mary Lindquist
Eugene Maier
Lourdes Monteagudo
Elizabeth Phillips
Thomas Post

Table of Contents

Additional student pages may be found in the *Adventure Book* or the *Unit Resource Guide*.

Table of Contents

Additional student pages may be found in the *Adventure Book* or the *Unit Resource Guide*.

Letter to Parents

Dear Parents,

Math Trailblazers™ is based on the ideas that mathematics is best learned through solving many different kinds of problems and that all children deserve a challenging mathematics curriculum. The program provides a careful balance of concepts and skills. Traditional arithmetic skills and procedures are covered through their repeated use in problems and through distributed practice. *Math Trailblazers,* however, offers much more. Students using this program will become proficient problem solvers, will know when and how to apply the mathematics they have learned, and will be able to clearly communicate their mathematical knowledge. Computation, measurement, geometry, data collection and analysis, estimation, graphing, patterns and relationships, mental arithmetic, and simple algebraic ideas are all an integral part of the curriculum. They will see connections between the mathematics learned in school and the mathematics used in everyday life. And, they will enjoy and value the work they do in mathematics.

The *Student Guide* is only one component of *Math Trailblazers.* Additional material and lessons are contained in the *Adventure Book* and in the teacher's *Unit Resource Guides.* If you have questions about the program, we encourage you to speak with your child's teacher.

This curriculum was built around national recommendations for improving mathematics instruction in American schools and the research that supported those recommendations. The first edition was extensively tested with thousands of children in dozens of classrooms over five years of development. In preparing this second edition, we have benefited from the comments and suggestions of hundreds of teachers and children who have used the curriculum. *Math Trailblazers* reflects our view of a complete and well-balanced mathematics program that will prepare children for the 21st century—a world in which mathematical skills will be important in most occupations and mathematical reasoning will be essential for acting as an informed citizen in a democratic society. We hope that you enjoy this exciting approach to learning mathematics and that you watch your child's mathematical abilities grow throughout the year.

Philip Wagreich

Philip Wagreich
Professor, Department of Mathematics, Statistics, and Computer Science
Director, Institute for Mathematics and Science Education
The *Math Trailblazers* Team
Teaching Integrated Mathematics and Science (TIMS) Project
University of Illinois at Chicago

Unit 1
Welcome to Second Grade

	Student Guide	Adventure Book	Unit Resource Guide*
Lesson 1			
Hundreds of Coins			◎
Lesson 2			
Birth Months	◎		
Lesson 3			
Animals Galore	◎		
Lesson 4			
Animal Trading Cards	◎		
Lesson 5			
Addition Facts Strategies	◎		

Unit Resource Guide pages are from the teacher materials.

Ms. Carter's Class

Ms. Carter's class used the information in the data table to make a graph. Use the graph to answer questions on the following page.

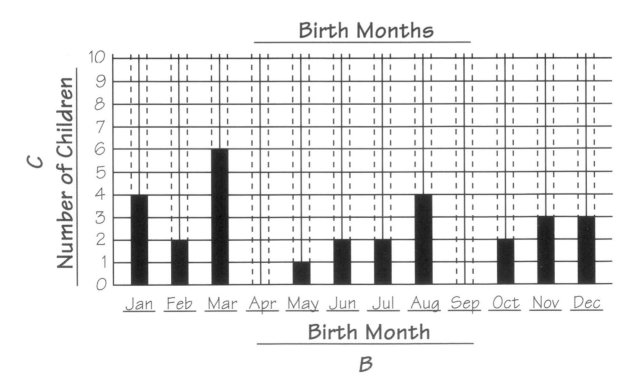

1. What is the most common birth month in Ms. Carter's class? How do you know?

_____

_____

2. What is the least common birth month? _____

3. How many children have birthdays in August? _____

4. Which months have the same number of birthdays?

_____

5. How many students are in Ms. Carter's class? _____

6. Is Ms. Carter's class larger, smaller, or the same size as your class? How do you know?

_____

_____

7. How is your class graph different from Ms. Carter's class graph?

_____

_____

_____

Animal Problems

1. Five kittens are playing with a ball of string. Three kittens are eating.

   How many kittens are in the litter? _____

2. A pod of whales has 3 males and 9 females.

   How many whales are in the pod? _____

3. A pig has 9 piglets in her litter. She already fed five of the piglets, and the rest are hungry.

   How many hungry piglets are there? _____

4. A pack of wolves has 5 adults and 8 pups.

   How many wolves live in this pack? _____

5. There was a herd of elephants. Three baby elephants were born. Now there are seven elephants.

   How many elephants were in the herd to start? _____

6. There were 11 chattering monkeys. Four fell asleep.

   How many monkeys are still chattering? _____

7. There were 12 toads sitting near the pond. Some jumped away. Four toads are still sitting near the pond.

   How many toads jumped away? _____

Name _____ Date _____

Animal Trading Cards

 Pod of Whales **4¢**

 Troop of Monkeys **5¢**

 Pride of Lions **6¢**

 Parliament of Owls **7¢**

 Pod of Whales **4¢**

 Troop of Monkeys **5¢**

 Pride of Lions **6¢**

 Parliament of Owls **7¢**

 Pod of Whales **4¢**

 Troop of Monkeys **5¢**

 Pride of Lions **6¢**

 Parliament of Owls **7¢**

Animal Trading Cards Problems

Pod of Whales	Troop of Monkeys	Pride of Lions	Parliament of Owls
4¢	5¢	6¢	7¢

Solve the problems. Write a number sentence for each.

1. Michelle bought a Pod of Whales card and a Pride of Lions card. How much did she spend?

   _____

2. Loni bought two Pride of Lions cards. How much did she spend?

   _____

3. Katrina spent 13¢. What did she buy?

   _____

4. Freddie spent 9¢. What did he buy?

   _____

5. Tony bought a Pod of Whales card, a Troop of Monkeys card, and a Parliament of Owls card. How much did he spend?

   _____

More Animal Trading Cards Problems

Work with your partner to solve the problems. Write number sentences for each. Use your trading cards and counters to help you.

Pod of Whales	Troop of Monkeys	Pride of Lions	Parliament of Owls
4¢	5¢	6¢	7¢

1. Lowell bought 2 cards. Both of the cards are the same. He spent 14¢. What did he buy?

_____

2. Bill bought 2 different cards. He spent 11¢. What did he buy? Find 2 solutions.

_____

3. Martina had 10¢. She bought 2 cards. She can buy more than one of each card. What can she buy? Find 2 solutions.

_____

4. Sara bought 3 cards and spent 15¢. She can buy more than one of each card. What can she buy? Find 2 solutions.

_____

Different Solutions

Pod of Whales	Troop of Monkeys	Pride of Lions	Parliament of Owls
4¢	5¢	6¢	7¢

Shanta bought three cards and spent 18¢. Find as many solutions as you can. Write a number sentence for each. She can buy more than one of each card. Use counters and your trading cards to help you.

_____

_____

_____

Name _____ Date _____

Empty Ten Frames

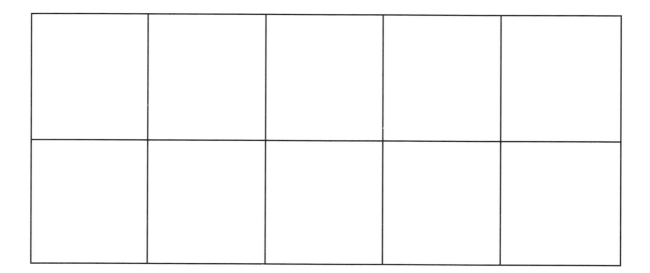

Ten Frames

Cut along the dotted lines.

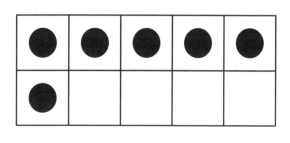

14

Cut along the dotted lines.

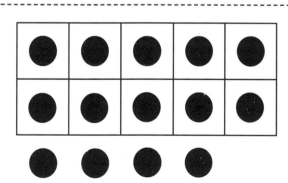

Double Ten Frames

Write two number sentences for each pair of ten frames.

Two number sentences for the ten frames on the right are

$$9 + 6 = 15$$
and
$$5 + 5 + 4 + 1 = 15$$

1. _____

_____

2. _____

_____

3. _____

_____

4. _____

_____

5. _____

_____

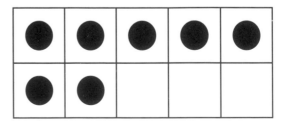

Unit 2

Exploring Numbers

	Student Guide	Adventure Book	Unit Resource Guide*
Lesson 1			
Tile Designs			
Lesson 2			
Exploring the *200 Chart*			
Lesson 3			
My Favorite			
Lesson 4			
Check It Out!			
Lesson 5			
Subtraction Facts			
Lesson 6			
Cover Up			
Lesson 7			
The Zoo Gift Shop			

Unit Resource Guide pages are from the teacher materials.

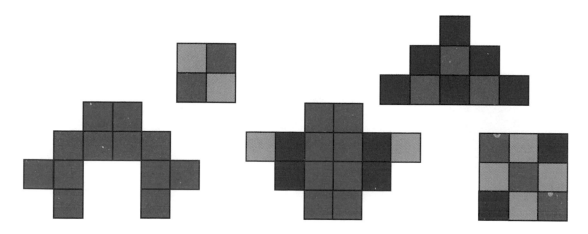

What's My Number Sentence?

Write two number sentences for each tile design.

1. A. _____

   B. _____

2. A. _____

   B. _____

3. A. _____

   B. _____

4. A. _____

   B. _____

5. A. _____

   B. _____

Make Your Own Tile Design

Make a design on the grid with tiles. Record your design by removing the tiles and coloring the squares.

Write your number sentences on a separate sheet of paper.

Miko's Tile Design

Miko made this design using color tiles. She wrote this number sentence to describe it.
1 + 2 + 3 + 2 + 1 = 9

Her friend Amy wrote another number sentence for the design. 1 + 3 + 5 = 9

1. Tell how Miko and Amy were looking at the design when they wrote these number sentences.

Miko

_____

_____

Amy

_____

_____

2. Write a different number sentence to describe Miko's design.

_____

Building a 200 Chart

1	2	3	4		6	7		9	10
11	12			15		17			20
		23					28	29	
31			34						40
		43				47			
	52						58		
				65		67			
	72				76				
81									90
91			94					99	100
			104					109	
	112					117			
					126			129	
131				135					140
	142						148		
			154		156				
	162							169	
171				175					
181			184			187			
191	192	193	194	195	196	197	198	199	200

200 Chart

1	2	3	4	5	6	7	8	9	10
11	12	13	14	15	16	17	18	19	20
21	22	23	24	25	26	27	28	29	30
31	32	33	34	35	36	37	38	39	40
41	42	43	44	45	46	47	48	49	50
51	52	53	54	55	56	57	58	59	60
61	62	63	64	65	66	67	68	69	70
71	72	73	74	75	76	77	78	79	80
81	82	83	84	85	86	87	88	89	90
91	92	93	94	95	96	97	98	99	100
101	102	103	104	105	106	107	108	109	110
111	112	113	114	115	116	117	118	119	120
121	122	123	124	125	126	127	128	129	130
131	132	133	134	135	136	137	138	139	140
141	142	143	144	145	146	147	148	149	150
151	152	153	154	155	156	157	158	159	160
161	162	163	164	165	166	167	168	169	170
171	172	173	174	175	176	177	178	179	180
181	182	183	184	185	186	187	188	189	190
191	192	193	194	195	196	197	198	199	200

Moving on the 200 Chart

To play this game, you and your partner need:

- A spinner;
- A scorecard;
- A *200 Chart.*

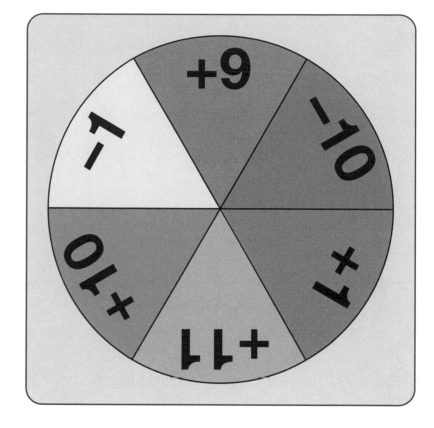

Directions

Begin at 50 on the *200 Chart*. Spin, and do what the spin tells you. Record your spin and your new number on your scorecard. Take turns with your partner until your scorecard is full. The partner with the biggest number at the end wins!

Moving on the 200 Chart
Scorecard

Player 1 _____

Start with 50.

Spin	New Number

Player 2 _____

Start with 50.

Spin	New Number

Spin and Add Playing Board

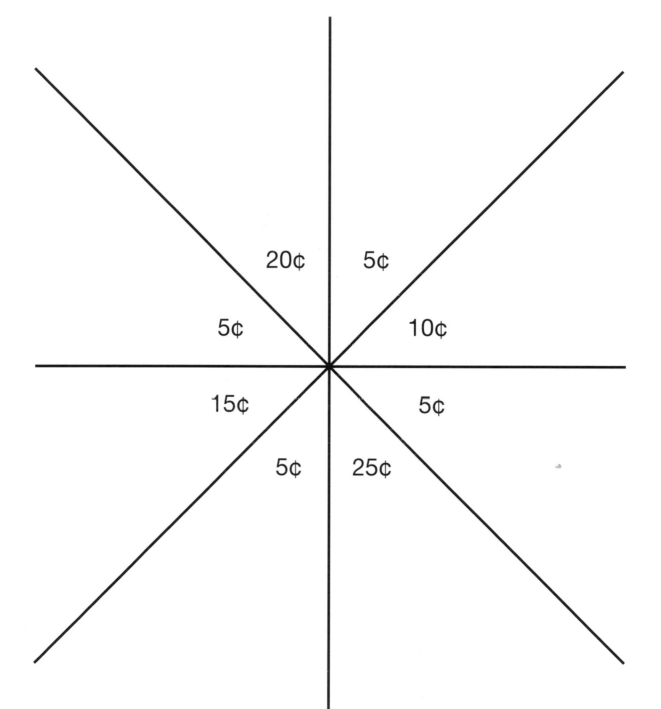

Spin and Add Score Sheet

Each player records the sum of three spins for each round. Player 1 and 2 compare their sums. The player with the higher sum gets one point. If the sums are the same, both players get one point.

	Sums		Points	
	Player 1	Player 2	Player 1	Player 2
Round 1				
Round 2				
Round 3				
Round 4				
Round 5				
Round 6				
Round 7				

Total _____ _____

Missing 200 Chart Numbers

Homework

Write the missing numbers in the pieces of the *200 Chart* below.

1	2	3
11	**12**	13
21	**22**	23

Example

	27	
		38

	73	
	83	

78		
	89	

Mr. Hart's Class

Mr. Hart's class used the information in the data table to make a graph.

Our Favorite Taco

T Type of Taco	C Number of Children
Steak	6
Chicken	7
Beef	9
Pork	0
Veggie	2
Avocado	3

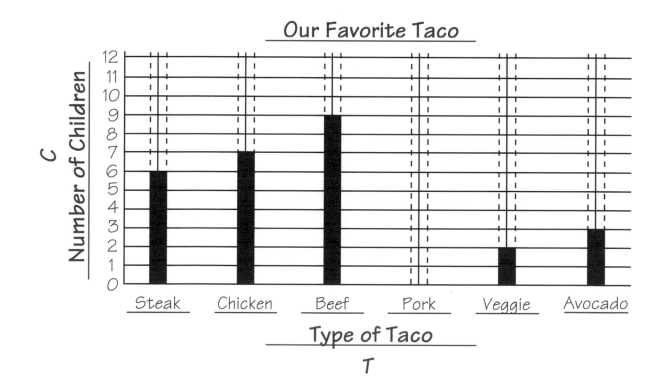

Our Favorite Taco

1. What is the most popular type of taco in Mr. Hart's class? How do you know?

   _____

   _____

2. What type of taco is the least favorite?

   _____

3. How many children chose chicken tacos as their favorite?

   _____

4. How many students are in Mr. Hart's class?

   _____

5. Mr. Hart ordered one taco for each of his students. The cashier put the veggie and the avocado tacos in one bag. All of the steak tacos were placed in a second bag. Which bag has more tacos? How many more?

   _____

6. The day after Mr. Hart's class graphed this data, two new students were added to the class. Joe and Anita both chose pork tacos as their favorite. Change the data table and graph to show Joe and Anita's data.

Name _____   Date _____

Fun at the Carnival

Homework

Dear Family Member:

You can help your child solve these problems by reading the problems with your child, providing counters to use as problem-solving tools, and asking your child to share his or her strategies.

Thank you.

Solve these problems in the way that works best for you. Write number sentences for each question.

1. Frank and Luis saved their money to go to the carnival. Frank saved $15 and Luis saved $19. How much more money did Luis save than Frank?

2. Both boys waited in line for a ride on the Scrambler. Frank waited 11 minutes. Luis waited 5 minutes. How much longer did Frank have to wait than Luis?

3. Frank had 15 tickets. He paid 6 tickets to ride the roller coaster. How many tickets did Frank have left?

4. Luis bought 2 hotdogs for $1 each. He gave the hotdog seller $5. How much money did Luis get back in change?

5. Frank bought a box of Chocos Candies. The box had 14 candies. He gave 7 candies to Luis. How many candies did Frank have left?

40

More Fun at the Carnival

Solve these problems in the way that works best for you.
Use ten frames, counters, or connecting cubes. Write number
sentences for Questions 1–4.

1. Luis tried to win a bear for his sister at the ring toss.
He tossed 12 rings. 5 rings landed on the mark. How many
rings missed the mark?

2. It takes 9 rings on the mark to win a bear. How many more
rings does Luis need to land on the mark to win a bear for
his sister?

3. Luis and Frank wanted to take a ride together. The ride
cost 6 tickets for each boy. Frank had 4 tickets and Luis
had 5 tickets. How many more tickets did they need to go
on the ride?

4. When they got home, Luis
and Frank counted their
money. Luis had 7 nickels
and Frank had 13 nickels.
How many more nickels
did Frank have
than Luis?

5. How much money
did each boy have
at the end of
the day?

Cover Up

Total Number of Beans _____

Write number sentences to describe each cover up problem.

Number of Beans Showing	Number of Beans Covered	Number Sentence

44

Name _____ Date _____

Zoo Gift Shop Animal Figures

Fill in prices for the animals below.

Garage Sale Problems

Homework

Dear Family Member:

Your child is learning about money in class. Help him or her solve the garage sale problems below. Your child should write number sentences to describe each problem. For example, a comic book and two baseball cards cost 8 + 3 + 3 = 14¢.

Solve the problems below. Write a number sentence for each.

doll clothes for 14¢ a set	comic books for 8¢ each
stickers for 4¢ a sheet	markers for 9¢ each
lemonade for 7¢ a cup	baseball cards for 3¢ each

1. How much for one sticker and one comic book?

   _____

2. How much for a marker and a cup of lemonade?

   _____

3. How much change from a dime do you get if you buy a sticker and a baseball card?

   _____

4. You have 35¢. What can you buy? Write two number sentences.

   _____

Unit 3

Buttons: A Baseline Assessment Unit

	Student Guide	Adventure Book	Unit Resource Guide*
Lesson 1			
All Sorts of Buttons	◎		
Lesson 2			
A Handful of Buttons	◎		
Lesson 3			
Button Sizer	◎		
Lesson 4			
Addition with Triangle Flash Cards	◎		
Lesson 5			
Button Solutions	◎		
Lesson 6			
Button Place Value	◎		

Unit Resource Guide pages are from the teacher materials.

All Sorts of Buttons 1

List as many ways as you can to sort the buttons.

_____

_____

_____

_____

_____

_____

_____

_____

_____

_____

_____

All Sorts of Buttons 2

Draw

How I sorted my buttons:

How Would You Sort Them?

Sort the following buttons. Describe how you would sort them below.

_____

_____

_____

_____

_____

_____

_____

Handful of Buttons 1

Estimate the number of buttons in your handful. Group and count them.

Estimate	Groupings	Count

Handful of Buttons 2

There were _____ buttons in my handful.

I grouped them this way:

Class Data Table

Number of Buttons	Number of Children
0 – 9	
10 – 19	
20 – 29	
30 – 39	
40 – 49	
50 – 59	
60 – 69	
70 – 79	
80 – 89	
90 – 99	
	Total:

Button Sizer

Use the boxes to decide if your buttons are small, medium, or large.

If a button fits in this box, it is <u>small</u>.

If a button fits in this box but not in the small box, it is <u>medium</u>.

If a button does not fit in the medium box, it is <u>large</u>.

Size	Number of Buttons	Total
Small		
Medium		
Large		

Button Sizer Graph

Use the information from your data table to complete the following graph.

Graph of Buttons

Size

Button Sizer

Triangle Flash Cards: Group A

- Cut out the flash cards. To practice an addition fact, cover the corner with the highest number. (It is shaded.) Add the two uncovered numbers.

- Divide the cards into three piles: those facts you know and can answer quickly, those that you can figure out, and those that you need to learn.

- Practice the last two piles again. Then, make a list of the facts you need to practice at home.

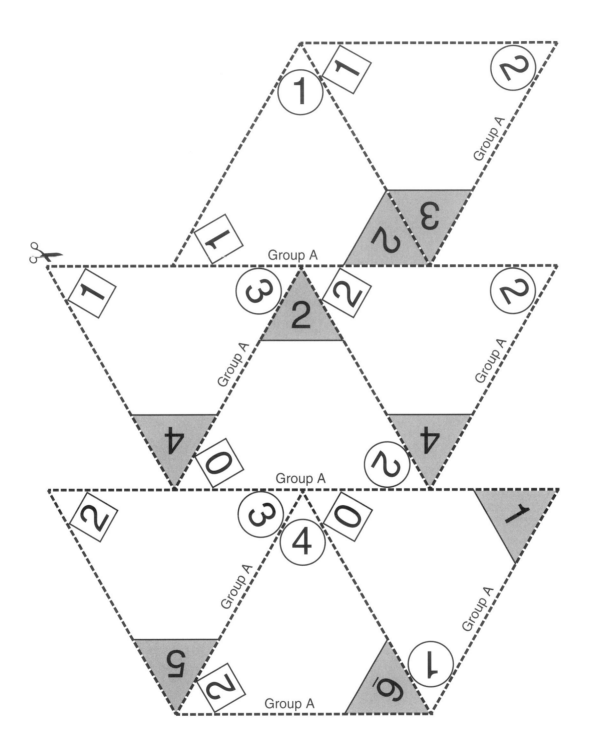

Addition with Triangle Flash Cards

Triangle Flash Cards: Note Home

Homework

Dear Family Member:

Your child is beginning a systematic study of the addition and subtraction facts. In each unit your child will study a small group of facts using *Triangle Flash Cards*. In this unit, your child will study the addition facts in Group A (0 + 1, 1 + 1, 2 + 1, 3 + 1, 0 + 2, 2 + 2, 3 + 2, 4 + 2). To help with the study of the facts, follow these directions.

- Choose a card and cover the corner with the largest number. It is shaded. Ask your child to add the two uncovered numbers.

3 + 1 = ?

1 + 3 = ?

- As you work through the cards, divide them into three piles: those facts your child knows and can answer quickly, those that your child can figure out, and those that your child needs to learn.

- Have your child make a list of the facts in the last two piles for further practice. Concentrate on the facts your child needs to learn.

- Discuss strategies that are useful for learning these facts.

- Practice the last two piles a second time.

- Help your child study these facts for a few minutes each day.

Thank you for your cooperation.

Button Solutions

Solve each problem. Show how you found the answer.

1. Julia grabbed a handful of buttons. She had 8 red, 6 blue, and 7 orange buttons. How many buttons were in her handful?

2. Sarah had 22 buttons in her collection. She gave 8 to Jeanette and 10 to Eric. How many buttons did she have left?

3. Stephen sorted some buttons into four groups of 5 and 2 buttons left over. How many buttons were in Stephen's handful?

4. Randy sorted some buttons into two groups of 10 and 7 buttons left over. How many buttons did Randy have?

Bertha's Button Boutique

At Bertha's Button Boutique, you can buy many different types of buttons. The following cards show you four different kinds.

Card A   Card B   Card C   Card D

   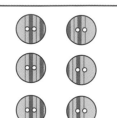

69¢   35¢   25¢   50¢

Solve each problem. Show how you found the answer.

1. Amanda bought Card A and Card B. How much did she spend?

_____

2. Rachel bought two Card Bs. How many buttons did she get?

_____

How much did Rachel spend?

_____

3. Adan likes the buttons on Card D. If he buys two Card Ds, how many buttons will he get?

_____

4. Thomas bought Card C and Card D. How much did he spend?

_____

Button Place Value Tables

My group counted these buttons:

Hundreds	Tens	Ones

My group counted _____ buttons.

Our class counted these buttons:

Hundreds	Tens	Ones

Our class has a total of _____ buttons.

Guess and Group

Homework

Dear Family Member:

In class, your child grabbed a handful of buttons, grouped them into piles of ten, and recorded the number of tens and buttons left over. Give your child a bowl filled with objects such as pennies, popcorn, cereal, or beads.

Thank you for your cooperation.

Take two handfuls from the bowl.

What object did you grab? _____

Estimate: I grabbed about _____ objects.

Tens	Ones

Group the objects into piles of ten. How many groups of ten do you have? How many ones are left over? Record your answers in the first row in the table.

Write a sentence describing your handfuls. Include the type of object and how many you grabbed.

_____

Ask a family member to take two handfuls. Estimate the number he or she pulled. Group the objects and complete the second row in the table. Then, record the actual number.

Estimate _____   Actual Number _____

Unit 4

Working with Data

	Student Guide	Adventure Book	Unit Resource Guide*
Lesson 1			
High, Wide, and Handsome	◉		
Lesson 2			
Are They Related?	◉		
Lesson 3			
How Do They Compare?	◉		◉
Lesson 4			
When Close Is Good Enough	◉		

*Unit Resource Guide pages are from the teacher materials.

High, Wide, and Handsome

Draw a picture of the lab. Be sure to show height (*H*) and arm span (*AS*).

Collect

Measure the height and arm span for each student in your group.

Name	H Height (in _____) unit	AS Arm Span (in _____) unit

1. What is the shortest arm span in your group?

_____

2. What is the tallest height in your group?

_____

3. What is the difference between the tallest height and the shortest height?

_____

Name _____   Date _____

Arm Span Graph

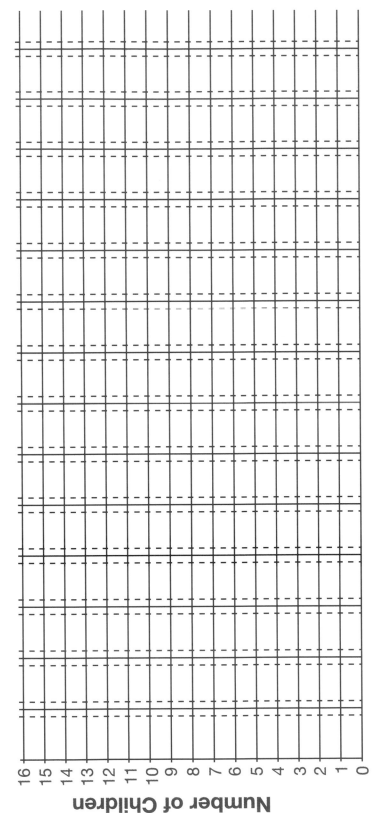

C
Number of Children

16
15
14
13
12
11
10
9
8
7
6
5
4
3
2
1
0

Arm Span (in links)
AS

Name _____ Date _____

Graph

Height Graph

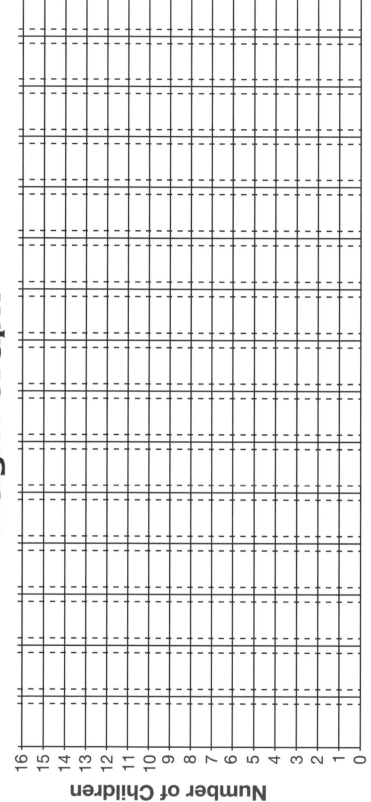

Height (in links)

H

Number of Children

C

16
15
14
13
12
11
10
9
8
7
6
5
4
3
2
1
0

Answer the following questions using the class data table.

4. Look at the tallest height and the shortest height. What is the range for height?

_____

5. Look at the longest arm span and the shortest arm span. What is the range for arm span?

_____

6. Maria's arm span is 33 links. How many links tall is Maria? Explain your thinking.

_____

_____

7. If you had identical twins in your class, would you expect their arm spans to be the same and their heights to be the same? Explain your thinking.

_____

_____

Colors of Shoes at My House

Homework

Dear Family Member:

Over the next few days, your child will collect and analyze data about the shoes in your home. As the assignment progresses, please help your child illustrate his or her data gathering, fill in the data table, make a graph, and answer the questions.

Thank you for your cooperation.

Choose three colors of shoes. Find the number of pairs of shoes of each color. Draw a picture that shows what you will do.

Collect

Fill in the table and graph with data collected at home.

C Colors of Shoes	P Number of Pairs

Graph

Color of Shoes

C

Answer the following questions based on your data table.

1. What is the most common shoe color?

_____

2. What is the least common shoe color?

_____

3. How many pairs of shoes are there?

_____

4. How many shoes are there altogether?

_____

5. What is the range for the number of pairs of shoes?

_____

Triangle Flash Cards: Group B

- Cut out the flash cards. To practice an addition fact, cover the corner with the highest number. (It is shaded.) Add the two uncovered numbers.

- Divide the cards into three piles: those facts you know and can answer quickly, those that you can figure out, and those that you need to learn.

- Practice the last two piles again. Then, make a list of the facts you need to practice at home.

High, Wide, and Handsome

Three Rectangles

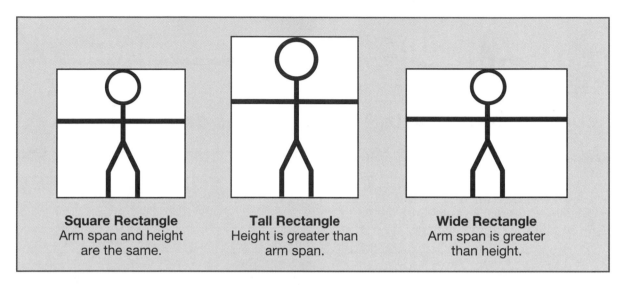

Square Rectangle
Arm span and height
are the same.

Tall Rectangle
Height is greater than
arm span.

Wide Rectangle
Arm span is greater
than height.

Complete the following sentences.

I am _____ links tall.

My arm span is _____ links.

The difference between my height and arm span is _____.

My height and arm span make a _____ rectangle shape.

Height and Arm Span Graph

Number the vertical axis. Then, graph the data.

L
Number of Links

Height
H

**Arm
Span**
AS

Type of Rectangle

Write the total of the tallies in the third column.

Miss Ozima's Class Rectangles

Type of Rectangle	Tallies	Total
Square Rectangle Arm span and height are the same.	卌 卌 |||	
Tall Rectangle Height is greater than arm span.	卌 卌 ||||	
Wide Rectangle Arm span is greater than height.	||	

Use the information from Miss Ozima's class to make a bar graph. Number the vertical axis by ones.

C
Number of Children

Square   Tall   Wide

Type of Rectangle
T

Making Comparisons

Use the graph to answer the question below.

How are the two data collections alike and how are they different? Make lists to show your findings.

Alike:

_____

_____

_____

_____

Different:

_____

_____

_____

_____

Hand Spans and Cubits

Measure each of the items listed below using your hand span. Then, measure them using your cubit. Measure two more objects or distances of your choice. Add them to the data table.

Object or Distance	Hand Spans	Cubits	
width of desk			
teacher's desk to door			
height of chalk rail			
teacher's desk to sharpener			
height of filing cabinet			

Choose a third measurement tool. Label the fourth column. Measure the objects and distances using this tool.

My Desk: Guess and Check

1. I estimate that the height of my desk is about

   _____ hand spans.

2. Measure the height of your desk using hand spans. My desk is about

   _____ hand spans.

3. Describe what you think about when you make an estimate.

   _____

   _____

   _____

4. I estimate that the height of my desk is about _____ cubits.

5. Measure the height of your desk using cubits. My desk is

   about _____ cubits.

6. Choose something else to measure in the room.

   My _____ is about _____ hand spans.

   My _____ is about _____ cubits.

Handy Measurements at Home

Homework

Dear Family Member:

Your child is learning to measure using his or her hand span and cubit. These units of measure are illustrated in the picture. Please help your child select some objects to measure and complete the assignment.

Thank you for your cooperation.

Hand span

Cubit

Measure three objects or distances with your hand span and cubit. Predict what a family member's measurements will be. Record his or her measurements and check your predictions.

Object or Distance	My Hand Spans	Prediction	Your Hand Spans
width of refrigerator			

Object or Distance	My Cubits	Prediction	Your Cubits
width of refrigerator			

Could Be or Crazy?

Circle whether each statement "could be" true or if it is "crazy."

1. Tasha measured her dog's tail. It was 2 hand spans long.

   Could Be   Crazy

2. Fred is a second-grader. He measured his height in cubits. He measured 30 cubits tall.

   Could Be   Crazy

3. Linda says her kitchen table is 4 cubits long. She says it is 4 hand spans long too.

   Could Be   Crazy

4. Connie said, "My hair is about 1 cubit long."

   Could Be   Crazy

5. Mark's dad says the width of the doorway is 5 hand spans. Mark, a second-grader, measured 3 hand spans.

   Could Be   Crazy

6. Choose one of the statements. Explain how you decided if it was a "could be" or a "crazy" statement.

   _____

   _____

   _____

Unit 5

GOING TO GREAT LENGTHS

	Student Guide	Adventure Book	Unit Resource Guide*
Lesson 1			
The Long and Short of It	@		
Lesson 2			
Exploring the Number Line	@		
Lesson 3			
Centimeters and Meters	@		
Lesson 4			
Rolling Along in Centimeters	@		
Lesson 5			
Mine Is the Best: The Challenge		@	

Unit Resource Guide pages are from the teacher materials.

Measurement Interval

Predict three objects that fit in each interval. Then, use a chain of links to measure each length.

0–50 Links

Object	Length (in links)

51–100 Links

Object	Length (in links)

101–150 Links

Object	Length (in links)

Triangle Flash Cards: Group C

- Cut out the flash cards. To practice an addition fact, cover the corner with the highest number. (It is shaded.) Add the two uncovered numbers.

- Divide the cards into three piles: those facts you know and can answer quickly, those that you can figure out, and those that you need to learn.

- Practice the last two piles again.

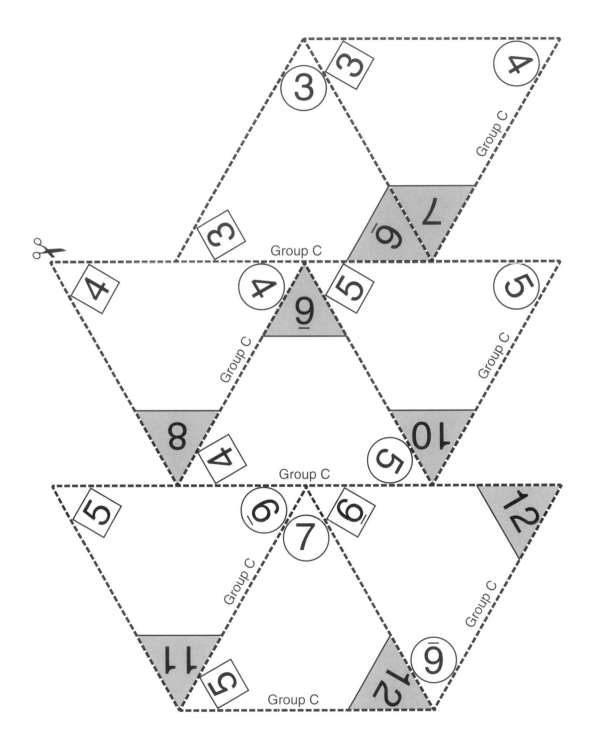

What's My Location?

Fill in the missing numbers on each number line.

A.

0 1 2 3 4 _ _ 6 7 8 9 _ _ 11 12

B.

25 26 27 _ _ 30 31 _ _ 36 37 38

C.

90 91 92 _ _ _ 98 _ _ 101 _ _ 103

D.

44 46 48 50 52 54 56 58 60

E.

20 _ 25 _ 30 _ 35

Number Lines

As your teacher calls out numbers, write them on the number line.

A.

0   10   20   30   40   50

B.

50   60   70   80   90   100

C.

0   20   40

D.

0   5   10   15   20   25   30   35   40   45   50

E.

Name _____ Date _____

Number Line for Heights

Find the height in inches of each of your family members. Record the numbers on the number line.

Name _____

Date _____

My Own Number Line

0   20   40   60   80   100

My number is _____. Place the number on the number line.

I know it goes where I put it because _____

_____

_____

_____

_____

_____

_____

_____

Building a Meter Tape

Centimeters and Meters

Measuring Small Objects

Use your meter tape or a meterstick.

1. How wide is your index finger? _____ cm

2. How long is the pencil? _____ cm

3. How long is this paper? _____ cm

4. Your choice: _____ _____ cm
item name

Measuring Big Objects

Use your paper meter tape or a meterstick.

1. How high is your desk?

   _____ cm

2. How tall are you? Have a classmate help measure your height.

   _____ cm

3. Are you exactly one meter tall?

   _____

4. Are you taller or shorter than one meter?

   _____

5. How high is it from the windowsill to the floor?

   _____ cm

   Is this exactly one meter? _____

   Is this more or less than one meter?

   _____

Estimating and Measuring

Find objects in the room. Estimate their lengths. Then, measure them.

Centimeters

Object	Estimation (centimeters)	Measurement (centimeters)
Eraser	5 cm	3 cm

Meters and Centimeters

Object	Estimation (m and cm)	Measurement (m and cm)

10-centimeter Treasure Hunt

Homework

Dear Family Member:

Your child is learning to estimate and measure length. Help your child complete the problems below.

Thank you for your cooperation.

Use your paper meter tape. Look for objects that measure close to 10 centimeters. List the name of each object you find.

1. _____

2. _____

3. _____

4. _____

5. _____

Challenge:

Find objects or distances that measure close to 1 meter. List the name of each object or distance you find.

1. _____

2. _____

Tony at the Ballpark

Tony wrote the following story about measurements.

"My uncle took me to a baseball game. The White Sox played the Yankees. The ballpark was so big! We walked 80 **centimeters** to get to our seats. I bought a large soda about 1 **meter** tall and a hot dog 20 **centimeters** long. The food was great! A White Sox player hit a home run. The ball must have gone 100 **centimeters!** A fan with a baseball glove 1 **meter** wide caught the ball. It was a wonderful day."

Complete the table using Tony's measurements. Which ones "could be" correct measurements, and which are "crazy"?

Object or Distance	Measurement	Could Be or Crazy
walk to seats		
large soda		
hot dog		
home run		
baseball glove		

Change Tony's story so it makes sense.

_____

Rolling Along in Centimeters

Draw a picture to show how you will set up the lab. Be sure to show the two main variables.

What two main variables are we studying in this lab?

_____

What should stay the same each time the car is rolled?

_____

_____

Collect

Work with your group to test each car. Record your data in the table below.

T Type of Car	**D** Distance in _____ *unit*			
	Trial 1	Trial 2	Trial 3	Median
Sample				

Make a bar graph of your data.

1. A. Which car rolled the longest distance?

_____

D = _____

B. Which car rolled the shortest distance?

_____

D = _____

C. What is the difference between the longest and the shortest distances? Show how you found your answer.

_____

2. You want to see which car is the best roller in the class. Can you tell using only your group's data table? Why or why not?

_____

_____

3. The teacher asked Debbie how far her car rolled. "It rolled 132," Debbie said. What is wrong with Debbie's answer?

_____

_____

Franco's Data

Franco's team found the data shown in the graph below.

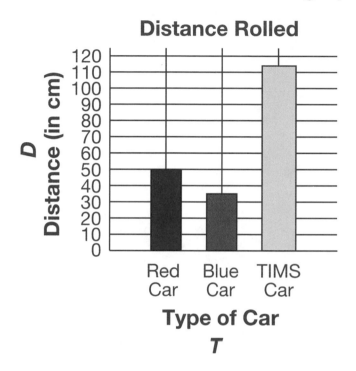

Distance Rolled

1. How far did the TIMS car roll?

   _____

2. How much farther did the TIMS car roll than the Red Car?
   Tell how you know.

   _____

   _____

3. Name at least one other thing you know by reading
   this graph.

   _____

   _____

Thumbs Up

Homework

Dear Family Member:

Your child is learning to measure with a meter tape. The thumb measurement should be taken from the tip to the base of the thumb (the second knuckle). Assist your child in measuring each of his or her fingers as well as those of a family member. Use the paper meter tape your child made in school or a ruler that indicates centimeters.

Measure the thumbs of family members. Write the measurements in the table.

Family Member	Thumb Length (in centimeters)

My Finger Measurements

1. Thumb _____ cm

2. Index _____ cm

3. Middle _____ cm

4. Ring _____ cm

5. Little _____ cm

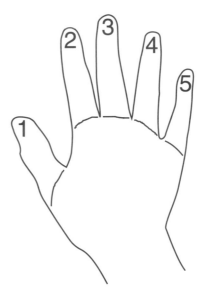

Choose a family member. Do you think his or her fingers will be the same, longer, or shorter than your fingers?

_____

Measure and find out.

My _____'s Finger Measurements

1. Thumb _____ cm

2. Index _____ cm

3. Middle _____ cm

4. Ring _____ cm

5. Little _____ cm

Rolling Along in Centimeters

Rolling Cars: Partner Problems

Homework

Two cars rolling down the ramps are shown below. In this drawing, we are looking down from above.

Ramp

A

| 10 20 30 40 50 60 70 80 90 100 | 10 20 30 40 50 60 70 80 |
| cm | cm |

1st Meterstick   **2nd Meterstick**

Ramp

B

1. How far did Car A roll? _____

2. How far did Car B roll? _____

3. How much farther did Car B roll than Car A? Show how you found your answer.

_____

_____

4. Did Car B roll twice as far as Car A? How do you know?

_____

_____

Unit 6

PUTTING NUMBERS IN THEIR PLACES

	Student Guide	Adventure Book	Unit Resource Guide*
Lesson 1			
Take Your Time	◉		
Lesson 2			
Pasta Place Value	◉		
Lesson 3			
Every Number Has Its Place	◉		◉
Lesson 4			
Take Your Places, Please	◉		
Lesson 5			
Marshmallows and Containers	◉		
Lesson 6			
The Princess and Her Playmate		◉	

Unit Resource Guide pages are from the teacher materials.

Name _____ Date _____

Make Your Own

Cut out the clocks and hands below.

HOURS   MINUTES

HOUR HAND   MINUTE HAND
MINUTE HAND   HOUR HAND

Cut out each strip. Cut only on the dotted lines.

HOURS		MINUTES	
1	7	00	30
2	8	05	35
3	9	10	40
4	10	15	45
5	11	20	50
6	12	25	55

Name _____ Date _____

Clocks

Write the times on the clocks below.

1.

_____

2.

_____

3.

_____

4.

_____

5.

1:00

6.

4:00

7.

7 o'clock

8.

12 o'clock

Just a Minute

Write the times on the clocks below.

1.

_____

2.

_____

3.

_____

4.

_____

5.

3:35 _____

6.

7:55 _____

7.

_____

"It's four fifteen."

8.

_____

"It's nine twenty."

Triangle Flash Cards: Group D

- Cut out the flash cards. To practice an addition fact, cover the corner with the highest number. (It is shaded.) Add the two uncovered numbers.

- Divide the cards into three piles: those facts you know and can answer quickly, those that you can figure out, and those that you need to learn.

- Practice the last two piles again. Then, make a list of the facts you need to practice at home.

1   8   7   2   8

Group D   Group D

7   2   10   9

Group D

3   9   10   3   8   8

Group D   Group D

9   3   7   11   1   9

Group D   Group D

4   9   7   4   12

Group D   Group D

10   4   11   8

Group D

Name _____   Date _____

Place Value Mat

134

Name _____ Date _____

Place Value Recording Sheet

Bundles of One Hundred	Stacks of Ten	Leftovers

Professor Peabody's Problems

Solve the following problems with connecting cubes.

1. Nell and Ross each bought a bag of pasta. They showed the number of pasta pieces in their bags with connecting cubes.

Professor Peabody said, "Nell's bag has more because it has nine loose cubes and Ross's only has one."

Is Professor Peabody right? _____
Explain how you know.

2. Clarissa has 32 pasta pieces. Melvin has 19. They showed their pieces with connecting cubes.

Professor Peabody said, "Melvin has more because he has 10 pieces and Clarissa only has 5." How would you help Professor Peabody? Explain.

3. Tracy found a bag of pasta and wanted to model the number. There were 109 pieces in the bag. Professor Peabody used connecting cubes to model the number. Did Professor Peabody model 109 correctly?

_____

Hundreds	Tens	Ones

Explain how you know.

_____

Draw a correct model for 109 pieces.

　　　　　　　　　　　　Pasta Place Value

Not More Than 100

Goal

To get as close to 100 cubes as possible in exactly five spins without going over.

Materials

- a pencil with paper clip for a spinner
- connecting cubes grouped in ones and tens

Directions

1. Make a chart like this one.

2. Spin five times. (All players share the same five spins.)

3. Each time the group spins, players take either that number of ones or tens from the pile of cubes. Then, players record the number taken on their charts.

   Example: A spin is 5. You can take 5 ones and record 5 **or** you can take 5 tens and record 50.

4. The player who has the most connecting cubes after five spins, but not more than 100, wins.

My Score

Spin	Tens	Ones
1		
2		
3		
4		
5		
Total		

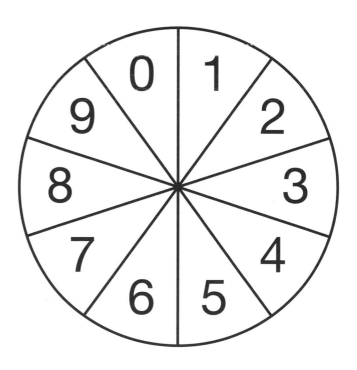

Matching Cubes and Numbers

Homework

Draw a line to match the models and the numbers.

1.

Bundles of 100	Stacks of 10	Leftovers
	1	2

2.

Bundles of 100	Stacks of 10	Leftovers
	3	6

3.

Bundles of 100	Stacks of 10	Leftovers
	4	4

4.

Bundles of 100	Stacks of 10	Leftovers
1	2	9

Draw pictures to represent the numbers or write a number to represent the given pictures.

5.

Bundles of 100	Stacks of 10	Leftovers
	1	5

6.

Bundles of 100	Stacks of 10	Leftovers
	2	3

7.

Bundles of 100	Stacks of 10	Leftovers

8.

Bundles of 100	Stacks of 10	Leftovers

Name _____

Date _____

Base-Ten Board

Flats	Skinnies	Bits

Base-Ten Recording Sheet

Flats	Skinnies	Bits

Base-Ten Numbers

Fill in the missing sections in the table.

	Number	One Way to Show Number
1.		
2.	23	
3.		
4.	85	
5.		

Fill in the missing sections in the table.

	Number	One Way to Show Number
6.	111	
7.		
8.	303	
9.		

Every Number Has Its Place

Building Numbers

Homework

A number is shown with base-ten pieces. In each problem, name the number and then write another way to make the number.

Example:

One Way			**Another Way**		
Flats	Skinnies	Bits	Flats	Skinnies	Bits
				11	13

Number ___123___

1.

One Way			**Another Way**		
Flats	Skinnies	Bits	Flats	Skinnies	Bits

Number _____

One Way

	Flats	Skinnies	Bits
2.		▯▯▯▯▯▯▯▯▯	▫▫▫▫▫

Another Way

Flats	Skinnies	Bits

Number _____

One Way

	Flats	Skinnies	Bits
3.	▦	‖	▫ ▫

Another Way

Flats	Skinnies	Bits

Number _____

One Way

	Flats	Skinnies	Bits
4.	▦	▯▯▯▯▯▯	▫▫▫▫▫

Another Way

Flats	Skinnies	Bits

Number _____

Take Your Places, Please
Game Rules

1. Agree with your partner to make the largest or the smallest number.

2. Draw the top card from your digit card deck.

3. Place the card in a frame on the digit mat.

4. Repeat steps 2 and 3.

5. Record the number on the Place Value Chart.

6. Compare your number with your opponent's number.

7. The winner records a tally point on the Place Value Chart.

8. Play ten rounds and add up tally points.

9. The person with the most tallies wins!

(You may use the discard frame if you draw four cards and throw one away. But, once a card is on the mat, it cannot be moved.)

Take Your Places, Please Digit Mat

Place your digit cards on the frames below to make the largest or the smallest number.

Discard

Name _____   Date _____

Digit Cards

Cut out the digit cards below. ✂

4	9
3	8
2	7
1	6
0	5

Place Value Chart

Record the numbers in the chart below. Mark a tally if you won the round.

Hundreds	Tens	Ones	Winning Tallies
		Total	

Name _____   Date _____

Marshmallows and Containers

Draw a picture of the experiment setup. Be sure to include the two main variables.

Collect

C Container	N Number of _____ unit

Make a graph of your data.

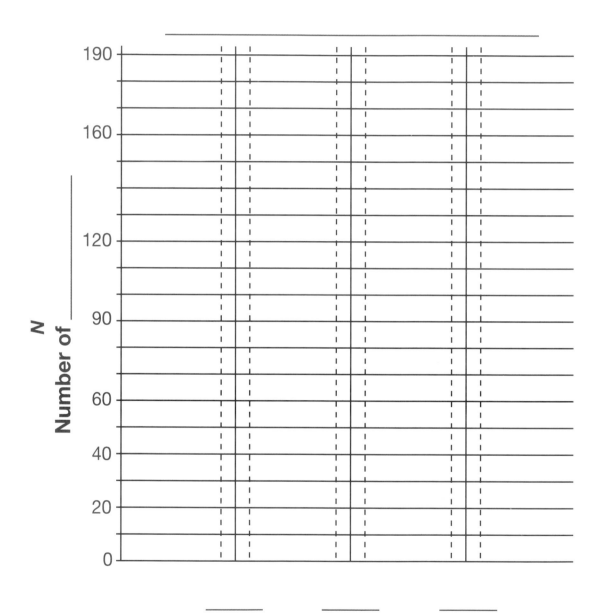

N
Number of _____

C
Container

Marshmallows and Containers

Explore

Use the data table and graph to answer the questions below.

1. What are the two main variables in this experiment?

_____

2. Which container is the tallest? _____

3. Which container is the widest? _____

4. Which container holds the most marshmallows? How do you know?

_____

_____

5. Which container has the largest volume? How do you know?

_____

_____

6. Which container has the smallest volume? Explain your answer.

_____

_____

Class Problem 1

Container D	**Container E**	**Container F**

Container D holds 62 beans.	Container E holds 43 beans.	Container F holds 29 beans.

1. Which container has the largest volume?

_____

2. Which container would have the largest volume if you used water instead of beans?

_____

3. Suppose the beans from Container D are poured into empty Container F. Will all the beans fit?

_____

If all the beans will not fit, how many beans will be left over? Tell how you know.

_____

_____

Class Problem 2

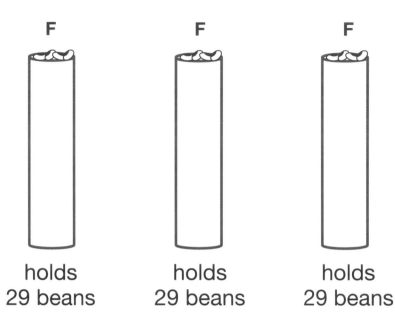

F

F

F

holds
29 beans

holds
29 beans

holds
29 beans

Container D
holds 62 beans.

Can an empty Container D hold all of the beans from the 3 filled
F containers? How can we find out?

_____

_____

_____

_____

Partner Problems

Michael and Shenika collected the data below. Use their data to answer the following questions.

Marshmallows and Containers

C Container	Number of $\frac{N \text{ Marshmallows}}{\text{unit}}$
tall	103
medium	170
short	110

1. How many more marshmallows can the medium container hold than the tall container? Tell how you found your answer.

_____

_____

_____

2. Can the beans from the tall and short containers fit into an empty medium container? Tell how you found your answer.

_____

_____

_____

Unit 7

Building with Cubes

	Student Guide	Adventure Book	Unit Resource Guide*
Lesson 1			
Cubes and Plans	◎		
Lesson 2			
Cube Model Plans	◎		◎
Lesson 3			
Architects in Cubeland	◎		◎
Lesson 4			
3-D Building Plans	◎		◎
Lesson 5			
Cube Model Problems	◎		

Unit Resource Guide pages are from the teacher materials.

Cube Model Pictures

Use words and pictures to show each shape you made using four connecting cubes.

Cube Model Twins

Look at the drawings of the cube models below. For each problem, circle the two drawings that have the *same shape.*

1.

2.

3.

Triangle Flash Cards: Group E

- Cut out the flash cards. To practice an addition fact, cover the corner with the highest number. (It is shaded.) Add the two uncovered numbers.

- Divide the cards into three piles: those facts you know and can answer quickly, those that you can figure out, and those that you need to learn.

- Practice the last two piles again. Then, make a list of the facts you need to practice at home.

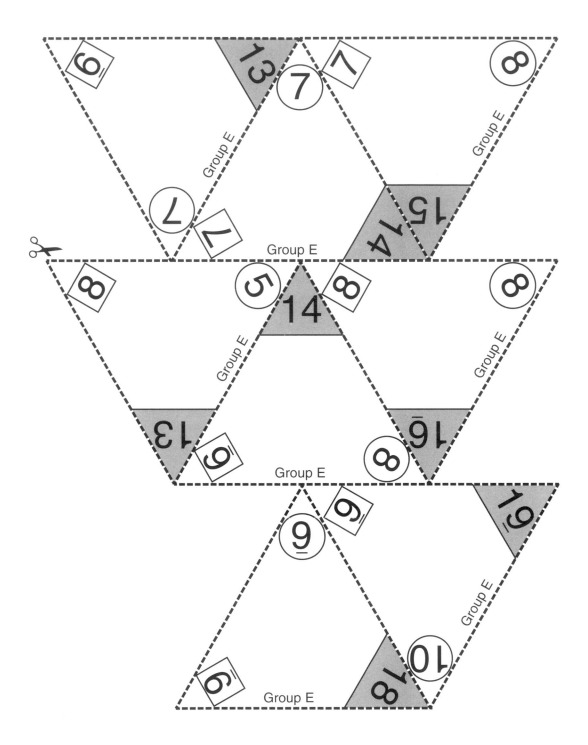

Sarah's Cube Models

Sarah made two cube models. Her plans are below.

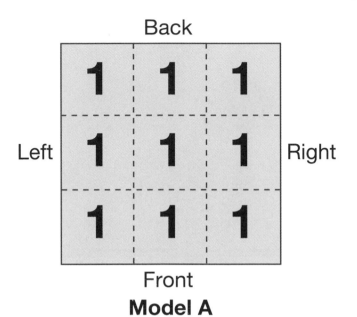

Back

Left | Right

Front
Model A

Make Sarah's cube models using her plans.

Discuss

Which model do you think is the biggest? Explain why.

_____

_____

_____

_____

_____

_____

_____

_____

_____

Back

Left | Right

Front
Model B

Sarah and Sebastian's Cube Tower Plan

Sarah and Sebastian used cubes to make a tower.

Sebastian, let's draw a plan to build a tower.

Write two different number sentences that describe the volume in cubic units.

_____

_____

Back

4	2	1
2	2	1
1	1	1

Left   Right

Front

Cube Model Plans

Galen's Cube Tower Plan

Use the plan below to build a tower that looks like the one Galen built.

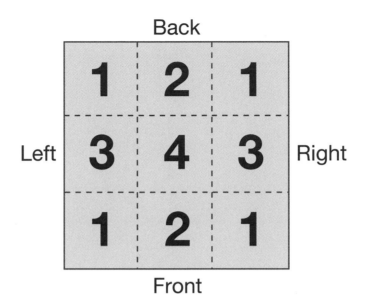

Back

Left | Right

Front

1	2	1
3	4	3
1	2	1

1. Ask your teacher to show you a model of Galen's tower. Does it look like yours?

_____

2. What is the volume of your tower?

_____

3. Write a number sentence to describe the volume in cubic units.

_____

_____

Name _____ Date _____

What If Volume Problems

Homework

Below are the cube model plans you used to build two towers.

Back

4	2	1
2	2	1
1	1	1

Left   Right

Front

**Sarah and Sebastian's
Cube Model Plan**

1. What is the volume of this model? _____

2. What if Sarah and Sebastian added one story to each column of their building? What will the new volume be?

   _____ Write a number sentence to describe

   the new volume in cubic units. _____

3. What if they made all the columns the same height as the tallest column? Write a number sentence to describe this

   volume in cubic units. _____

Below is Galen's Cube Model Plan.

Galen's Cube Model Plan

4. What is the volume of this model? _____

5. What if Galen added two stories to each column of his building? What would the new volume be?

_____ Write a number sentence to describe

the new volume in cubic units. _____

6. What if the center column of Galen's building was seven stories high instead of four stories high? Write a number sentence to describe this volume in cubic units.

_____

Cubeland Memo

Construct a building with cubes, and then make a plan.

Write a memo describing your new building to another architect team. Use the questions to write a description.

- How tall is the building?
- How long is the building from front to back?
- How many cubes make up the building?

Exchange the memo and your cube model plan with another team. Use the memo and the cube model plan to make a building that looks like the one that the other team built.

MEMO

TO: _____
names of student architects

FROM: _____
names of student architects

DATE: _____
month, day, year

Here is our team's description of our new building:

_____

_____

_____

What's the Volume?

Find the volume for the cube model plans and buildings.

1. _____ cubic units

2. _____ cubic units

3.

Back

4	4	2
2	4	4

Left   Right

Front

_____ cubic units

4.

Back

8	1
12	9

Left   Right

Front

_____ cubic units

City Buildings

Build cube models that look like the three drawings below. Find the volume of each building and write a number sentence to show your strategy.

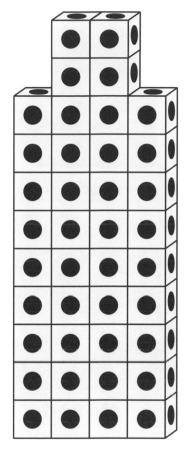

A. Quad City Towers

Volume _____

Number sentence _____

B. Six Corners Gym

Volume _____

Number sentence _____

Volume _____

Number sentence _____

C. Stair Step Apartments

City Buildings Match-Up

Which cube model goes with which cube plan? Draw a line from the plan to the matching model. Explain how you know.

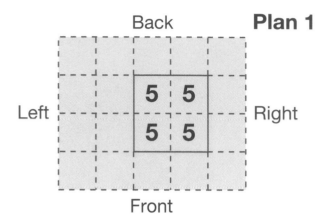

Back

Plan 1

Left   5 5
         5 5   Right

Front

Model A

Back

Plan 2

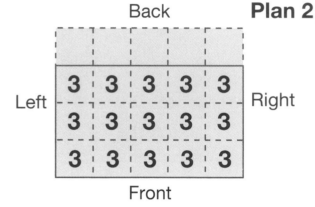

Left   3 3 3 3 3
         3 3 3 3 3   Right
         3 3 3 3 3

Front

Model B

Back

Plan 3

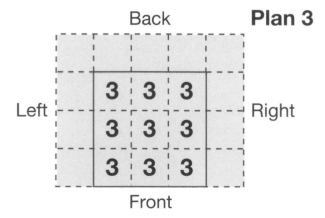

Left   3 3 3
         3 3 3   Right
         3 3 3

Front

Model C

Matching Plans with Models 1

Match the plan with the model, and connect them with a line. Find the volume of each model. Explain how you know.

Plan 1

Back

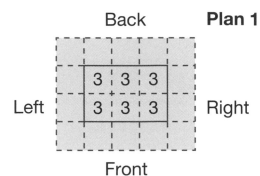

Left

Right

Front

Plan 2

Back

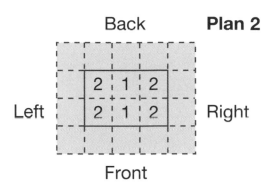

Left

Right

Front

Plan 3

Back

Left

Right

Front

Model A

Volume _____

Model B

Volume _____

Model C

Volume _____

Matching Plans with Models 2

Draw a line from the plan to the matching model. Find the volume of each model.

Plan 1

Back

3	3	2	1
2	2	2	1
1	1	1	1

Left   Right

Front

Model A

Volume _____

Plan 2

Back

1	2	3	4
1	2	3	4
1	2	3	4

Left   Right

Front

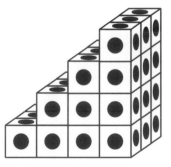

Model B

Volume _____

Plan 3

Back

			1
			1
			1
1	1	1	1	1

Left   Right

Front

Model C

Volume _____

Cube Model Problems

1. Use the following floor plans to make a cube model building with:

A. 9 cubes

Back

Left – – – – – – – – Right

Front

B. 11 cubes

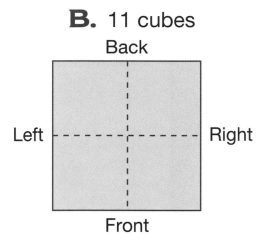

Back

Left – – – – – – – – Right

Front

C. 16 cubes

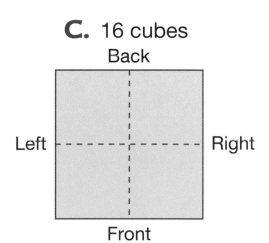

Back

Left – – – – – – – – Right

Front

2. Use the following floor plan to make a building out of 9 cubes.

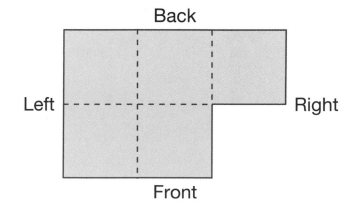

Back

Left – – – – – – – – Right

Front

More Cube Model Problems

Work with a partner to build a cube model that matches the clues in each problem. Make a record of your model on the cube model plan. You may find no solutions, one solution, or many solutions.

1. Clues

- The floor plan is a square with each side 2 units long.
- Volume = 8
- Height = 2

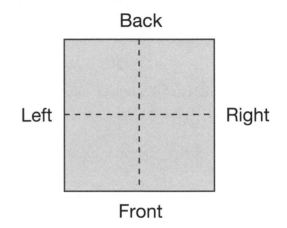

2. Clues

- The floor plan is a square with each side 2 units long.
- Volume = 6
- Height = 2

3. Clues

- The floor plan is a square with each side 2 units long.
- Volume = 9
- Height = 2

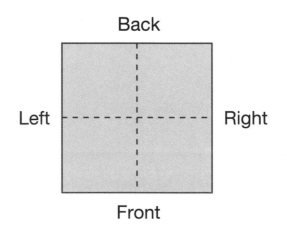

4. Clues

- The floor plan is a rectangle that is 3 units long and 2 units wide.

- Volume = 7

- Height = 2

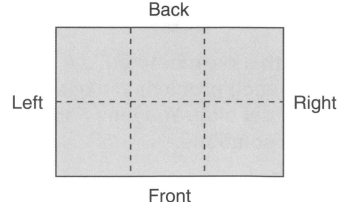

5. Make up your own cube model problem. Make sure you know the answer.

Clues

- The floor plan is a rectangle that is ____ units long

  and ____ units wide.

- Volume = ____   • Height = ____

6. Which of these problems have only one solution?

_____

7. Which of these problems have more than one solution?

_____

8. Which of these problems have no solution?

_____

Cube Model Challenge

> Dear Family Member:
>
> Your child is learning to build cube models and describe them using plans. Ask your child how he or she recorded plans in class. It will help if you imagine placing each 3-dimensional model on the grid.

Make a cube model plan from the drawing, *without using the cubes.*

Back

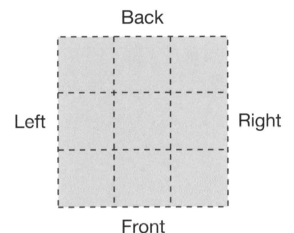

Left   Right

Front

Volume = _____

Back

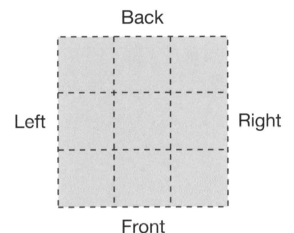

Left   Right

Front

Volume = _____

Cube Model Problems

Give Me a Clue

Read the clues for each problem. Build a cube model that solves each problem. Make a record of your model on the cube model plan.

1. Clues

- The floor plan is a square with each side 2 units long.

- Volume = _____

- Height = _____

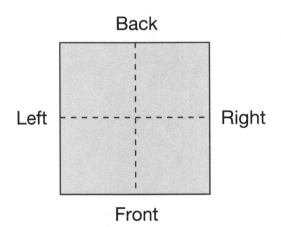

Back

Left · Right

Front

2. Clues

- The floor plan is a square with each side 2 units long.

- Volume = _____

- Height = _____

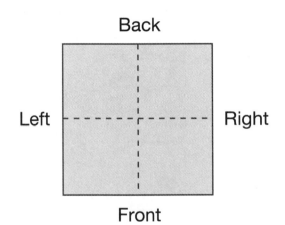

Back

Left · Right

Front

3. Clues

- The floor plan is shown at the right.

- Volume = _____

- Height = _____

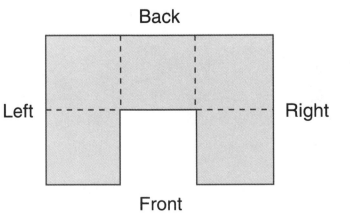

Back

Left · Right

Front

Unit 8
MULTIPLE MASSES

	Student Guide	Adventure Book	Unit Resource Guide*
Lesson 1			
Putting Masses in Order	◎		
Lesson 2			
The Mouse-Proof Shelf	◎	◎	
Lesson 3			
Measuring Mass	◎		◎

Unit Resource Guide pages are from the teacher materials.

Comparing Masses

Predict and line up objects from most mass to least mass. Draw and label the order of your objects.

Compare masses on the equal-arm balance. Record your results in the table.

Mass Comparison Data Table

Object in Pan 1	Object in Pan 2	More Mass

Analyzing Masses

Decide on the order of masses, and fill in the table below.

Mass Order Data Table

Mass Order	Name of Object
Most Mass	
↓	
Least Mass	

1. Which objects are the same size and shape?

_____

2. Do these two objects have the same mass? Why?

_____

3. Are the wood and steel spheres the same shape?

_____

4. Which is smaller: the wood or steel sphere? _____

5. Which has more mass: the wood or steel sphere? _____

6. Two new spheres are shown below. Which has more mass? Explain.

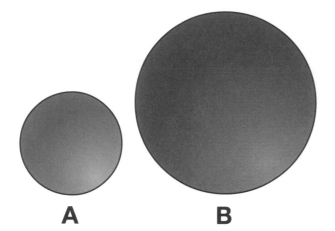

A   B

_____

_____

_____

_____

7. Cylinder A and Cylinder B are the same shape and size.

A   B

Mark the correct statement below.

_____ The masses are the same.

_____ Cylinder B has more mass.

_____ Cylinder A has more mass.

_____ You can't tell which has more mass.

Mass Hunt

Homework

Dear Family Member:

Your child is learning to find and compare the masses/weights of objects. Help your child search for two small objects at home that have similar masses/weights, but different shapes or sizes.

Thank you for your cooperation.

Draw the objects below and tell how you predict they have the same mass.

_____

_____

_____

Bring the two objects to school and check your predictions using the equal-arm balance.

Analyzing the Masses of Two Blocks

Here is a picture of two objects.

1. Do the objects have the same shape?

   _____

2. Are the objects the same size?

   _____

3. Can you tell which one has more mass? Explain.

   _____

   _____

A

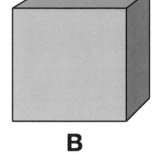

B

4. Block A and Block B are put on the balance. Does one of the pictures below show what will happen? Circle that picture.

Picture 1

Picture 2

Picture 3

_____ I can't tell what will happen.

Triangle Flash Cards: Group F

- Cut out the flash cards. To practice an addition fact, cover the corner with the highest number. (It is shaded.) Add the two uncovered numbers.

- Divide the cards into three piles: those facts you know and can answer quickly, those that you can figure out, and those that you need to learn.

- Practice the last two piles again. Then, make a list of the facts you need to practice at home.

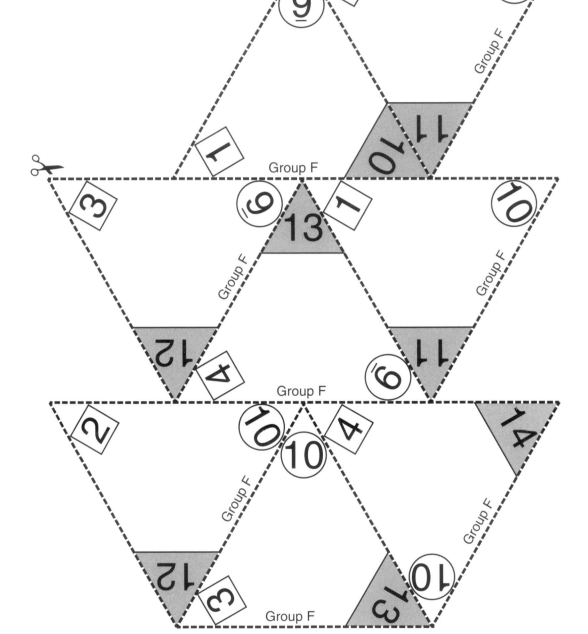

Putting Masses in Order

Millie, Minnie, Marty, and Mike Did It!

There are many possible combinations of masses for Millie and Mike, balancing Minnie and Marty on the hanging lamp. How many different combinations can you find?

Work with a partner. Pretend the mice can have any of these masses: 9 grams, 8 grams, 7 grams, 6 grams, 5 grams, 4 grams, 3 grams, 2 grams, or 1 gram. Each mouse has a different mass.

You can use connecting cubes to represent each mouse's mass to check your combinations on the equal-arm balance.

Record the combinations of masses in the tables on the next page.

Millie's and Mike's total mass should equal Minnie's and Marty's total mass. The first row shows an example.

Mouse Masses in Grams

Millie	Mike	Total	Minnie	Marty	Total
8	1	9	5	4	9

Measuring Mass

Draw a picture of the lab. Include the two main variables and the materials you will use.

Before you collect data, what must you do to the balance?

Collect

Find any object that is approximately 100 grams and 4 small objects to mass. Both partners should find the mass of each object on their own and then check each other's results.

Measuring Mass Data Table

N Name of Object	1 Gram	5 Grams	10 Grams	20 Grams	M Total Mass (in _____) unit

Graph

Make a bar graph of the data. Label both axes.

Measuring Mass

1. **A.** Which of your objects has the least mass?

   _____

   B. If you had four of these objects, would their combined mass be more than 100 grams or less than 100 grams?

   _____

   How did you figure it out?

   _____

   _____

   _____

2. **A.** Which of your objects has the most mass?

   _____

   B. Would three 40-gram objects have more mass or less mass than your heaviest object?

   _____

   How did you figure it out?

   _____

   _____

3. A. Find the sum of the masses of your heaviest object and your lightest object.

_____

B. Put these two objects in one balance pan and find their total mass. Did you get the same answer as in Question 3A? Why or why not?

_____

_____

_____

4.

| 1 | heaviest object | | lightest objects |

How many of your lighter objects come closest to balancing your heaviest object? How do you know?

_____

_____

_____

5. Bo uses these masses.

1 g	5 g	10 g	50 g
3	1	2	1

Object A

And the balance looks like this.

Then, Bo uses these masses.

1 g	5 g	10 g	50 g
4	1	2	1

Object A

And the balance looks like this.

Estimate the mass of Object A. _____

What's the Total Mass?

Homework

| Name _____ | Date _____ |

Dear Family Member:

Your child is learning to measure the mass of objects using an equal-arm balance. He or she places the object in one pan. In the other pan standard masses are placed until the two pans are balanced. Your child finds the total mass by adding up the values of the standard masses. Help your child complete the problems below.

In the following problems, Mary shows which masses she used to balance each object. What is the total mass of each object?

1. Eraser

_____

2. Meterstick

_____

3. Three pieces of chalk

_____

4. A sandwich

_____

Unit 9
Ways of Adding Larger Numbers

	Student Guide	Adventure Book	Unit Resource Guide*
Lesson 1			
In the Ballpark	@		
Lesson 2			
An Addition Seminar	@		
Lesson 3			
The Nameless Scribe	@	@	
Lesson 4			
Exploring with Base-Ten Pieces	@		
Lesson 5			
Adding with Paper and Pencil	@		
Lesson 6			
Snack Shop Addition	@		

Unit Resource Guide pages are from the teacher materials.

Price Cards

56¢	32¢	36¢	59¢
42¢	45¢	50¢	72¢
40¢	92¢	27¢	29¢
17¢	25¢	46¢	49¢
89¢	19¢	22¢	23¢

216

Which Is Closer?

Katen and Tamika mixed up their price cards and pulled some to estimate. Circle the "could be" estimates and cross out the "crazy" estimates. Give an estimate for the sum and tell how you made your estimate. An example is done for you.

Example:
Katen pulled a 72¢, a 27¢, and a 35¢ price card from the pile.

 ($1.50) $2.00 ($1.40) $5.00

Estimate the sum. _____$1.25_____

I used quarters for my estimate. 75¢ + 25¢ + 25¢ = $1.25.

1. Tamika pulled a 34¢, a 29¢, and a 26¢ card from the pile.

   90¢ $1.50   60¢ $1.00 $2.00

Estimate the sum. _____

_____

2. Katen and Tamika pulled a 56¢, a 31¢, a 65¢, and a 99¢ price card from the pile.

   $1.00 $2.00 $4.00 $2.75 $2.50

Estimate the sum. _____

_____

Numbers and Sense

Solve the following problems by estimating the sum. Each time, tell how you made your estimate.

1. Katen and Arlene went to a baseball game. They counted baseball caps. Arlene counted 27 caps and then 14 caps. Katen counted 32 caps and 48 caps. Estimate the number of caps they counted in all.

   _____

   _____

2. The hot dog vendor sold 68 hot dogs with ketchup, 2 hot dogs with mustard, and 9 plain hot dogs. Estimate the number of hot dogs sold.

   _____

   _____

3. The Chicago Cubs and the Chicago White Sox played a doubleheader. The Cubs had 22 hits in the first game and 13 hits in the second. The White Sox had 28 hits in the first game and 17 hits in the second. Estimate the number of hits in all.

   _____

   _____

Triangle Flash Cards: Group G

- Cut out the flash cards. To practice an addition fact, cover the corner with the highest number. (It is shaded.) Add the two uncovered numbers.

- Divide the cards into three piles: those facts you know and can answer quickly, those that you can figure out, and those that you need to learn.

- Practice the last two piles again. Then, make a list of the facts you need to practice at home.

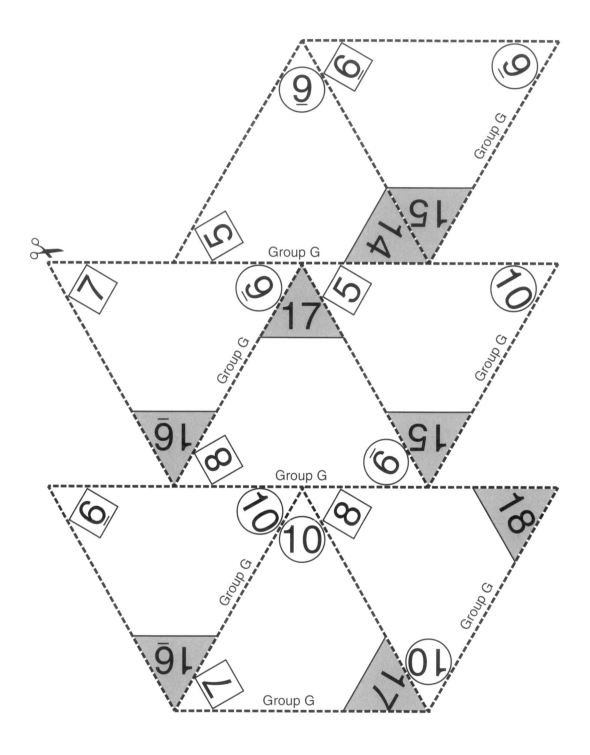

Computer Game Seminar

The Compute-with-Us Game Company held a seminar for school children. The students discussed new computer games. Help total the data collected at the seminar. Explain your thinking for each problem. Use words and pictures.

1. Twenty-nine students were from Chicago, Illinois, and thirty-three students were from Springfield, Illinois. How many students came from Illinois?

_____

_____

_____

2. In the morning session, the students named their favorite type of computer game. Fifty-five students liked sports games. Thirty-eight students liked space games. How many students were in the morning session?

_____

_____

_____

3. In the afternoon session, 54 students reported that space games were their favorite, 27 liked adventure games, and 32 liked sports games. Did more or less than 100 students attend the afternoon session?

_____

_____

_____

4. In the morning session, 46 students drew new characters they would like to see in a game. In the afternoon session, 36 students drew new characters. How many students drew new characters?

_____

_____

_____

5. Pretend you were at the seminar. What did you find out? Write a problem and find the answer.

_____

_____

_____

How Did They Do It?

Pretend you are a teacher, checking to see how your students solved this problem:

$$\begin{array}{r} 26 \\ + 58 \\ \hline \end{array}$$

Shanila showed her work like this:

$$\begin{array}{r} 26 \\ +58 \\ \hline 84 \end{array}$$

~~||||~~ ~~||||~~ ~~||||~~ ~~||||~~ ~~||||~~ |

~~||||~~ ~~||||~~ ~~||||~~ ~~||||~~ ~~||||~~ ~~||||~~ ~~||||~~ ~~||||~~ ~~||||~~ ~~||||~~ ~~||||~~ |||

What did she do to solve the problem?

Devon used the *200 Chart* and showed his work like this:

$$\begin{array}{r} 26 \\ +58 \\ \hline 84 \end{array}$$

26 36 46 56 66 76

77 78 79 80 81 82 83 84

What did he do?

Show another way to solve the problem on the back of this page.

Acme Grocery Store

H✿mework

Fill in the blank price tags with prices between 25¢ and 90¢.

Find the total cost for each problem and describe your thinking.

1. A can of soup and bar of soap cost _____.

_____

_____

2. A cheese wedge and a can of tuna cost _____.

_____

_____

3. A box of crackers and a box of tissues cost _____.

_____

_____

King Gupta's Feast

"We need one hundred fifty new golden plates, four hundred fifty flowers, three hundred one bananas, one hundred seventy cheeses, five hundred two sugar candies, and fifteen cakes," says King Gupta.

What should Krishna write down?

King Gupta requires _____ gold plates.	King Gupta requires _____ cheeses.
King Gupta requires _____ flowers.	King Gupta requires _____ candies.
King Gupta requires _____ bananas.	King Gupta requires _____ cakes.

Building Addition Problems

Before you do the problems below, estimate the answer. Use base-ten pieces to solve each problem, then explain how to do the problem another way.

1. The sum will be between _____ and _____.

$$\begin{array}{r} 15 \\ + 32 \\ \hline \end{array}$$

2. The sum will be between _____ and _____.

$$\begin{array}{r} 24 \\ + 58 \\ \hline \end{array}$$

3. The sum will be between _____ and _____.

$$\begin{array}{r} 65 \\ + 26 \\ \hline \end{array}$$

4. The sum will be between _____ and _____.

$$\begin{array}{r} 27 \\ 13 \\ + 55 \\ \hline \end{array}$$

What Happened Here?

Michael completed the following problem:

$$\begin{array}{r} 48 \\ + 49 \\ \hline 817 \end{array}$$

1. Is this a reasonable answer for this problem? How do you know?

_____

_____

2. What do you think Michael might have done?

_____

_____

3. How would you solve this problem? Make sure you explain your thinking.

_____

_____

Add to 100

Players: two or more

Materials: digit cards or regular playing cards, paper, pencil
(If you use the regular playing cards, only use the 1–9 cards.)

Winner: Player with the most cards at the end of the game.

Rules:

- Deal out four cards to each player.
- Each player uses the four cards to make an addition problem.
- Each player solves his or her addition problem.
- The player whose answer is closest to 100 takes everyone's cards and puts them aside.
- Keep dealing four more cards to each player and making problems.
- When all the cards are gone, the player who has collected the most cards wins.

Play several games. Then, write about what happened. Tell how you think you can win.

_____

_____

_____

_____

_____

Adding Two Ways

Homework

Solve the problems two ways. Show your thinking.

---

1. First way:

$$\begin{array}{r} 42 \\ +\ 49 \\ \hline \end{array}$$

---

2. Second way:

$$\begin{array}{r} 42 \\ +\ 49 \\ \hline \end{array}$$

Think It Through

Homework

Solve the following problems using paper-and-pencil addition. Show your thinking.

1. Jeremiah and Jordan collect baseball cards. Jeremiah has 56 Chicago White Sox cards. Jordan has 48 Chicago Cubs cards. If they combine their collections, how many Chicago cards will they have?

2. For his birthday, Jeremiah received 26 more White Sox cards to go with the 56 he already had. How many White Sox cards are now in his collection?

3. Jordan decided to collect Cardinal cards as well. He bought 35 cards to add to his collection of 48 cards. How many cards are now in his collection?

4.
$$\begin{array}{r} 25 \\ + 26 \\ \hline \end{array}$$

5.
$$\begin{array}{r} 68 \\ + 23 \\ \hline \end{array}$$

6.
$$\begin{array}{r} 45 \\ + 48 \\ \hline \end{array}$$

7.
$$\begin{array}{r} 52 \\ + 47 \\ \hline \end{array}$$

Shooting Star Snack Shop
Children's Menu

Food

Pizza Slice.................................. 79¢

Taco... 59¢

Grilled Cheese Sandwich............. 89¢

Turkey Sandwich.......................... 99¢

Peanut Butter and Crackers......... 49¢

Bagel.. 29¢

Potato Chips................................ 25¢

Pretzels.. 25¢

Brownie.. 35¢

Fruit Salad Cup........................... 65¢

Carrot Sticks................................ 29¢

Chicken Noodle Soup.................. 55¢

Chili.. 75¢

Drinks	Small	Medium	Large
Milk..............................	25¢	40¢	55¢
Lemonade.....................	39¢	55¢	79¢
Orange Juice................	55¢	70¢	85¢
Hot Chocolate..............	59¢	75¢	99¢

Snack Shop Bills

Shooting Star Snack Shop
You have up to $5.00 to spend.

Customer's Name:

Enrique

Item	Price(¢)
Grilled Cheese	89¢
Carrot Sticks	29¢
Chicken Noodle Soup	55¢
Brownie	35¢
Large Milk	55¢

Total is between

_____ and _____

Total _____

Is your total reasonable?

_____

Shooting Star Snack Shop

Customer's Name:

_____

Item	Price(¢)
_____	_____
_____	_____
_____	_____
_____	_____

Total is between

_____ and _____

Total _____

Is your total reasonable?

_____

Shooting Star Snack Shop
You have up to $2.00 to spend.

Item	Price(¢)
_____	_____
_____	_____
_____	_____
_____	_____
_____	_____

Customer's Name:

_____

Is your total reasonable?

Total _____   _____

Total is between

_____ and _____

Shooting Star Snack Shop
You have up to $3.50 to spend.

Item	Price(¢)
_____	_____
_____	_____
_____	_____
_____	_____
_____	_____

Customer's Name:

_____

Is your total reasonable?

Total _____   _____

Total is between

_____ and _____

Oops, I Spilled the Juice!

Splash Spiller and his friend, Nick, bought lunch at the Shooting Star Snack Shop. Unfortunately, Splash spilled juice on their bills so the prices of the specials, the homemade applesauce and banana bread, are blotted out.

Shooting Star Snack Shop Bill	
Customer's Name	_Splash_
Item	Price (¢)
Fruit Salad Cup	65¢
Pretzels	25¢
Cup of Applesauce	
Orange Juice	85¢
Total	$2.04

Shooting Star Snack Shop Bill	
Customer's Name	_Nick_
Item	Price (¢)
Chili	75¢
Taco	59¢
Banana Bread	
Medium Milk	40¢
Total	$2.23

How much did the applesauce cost?

How much did the banana bread cost?

Name _____ Date _____

Snack Shop Carryout

Homework

Make up your own problem on the bill below using your menu. If you ask family members or friends to place orders, you may use the space provided to list more items. Describe how you found your answer.

1.

Shooting Star Snack Shop

Item	Price(¢)	Customer's Name:
		_____
_____	_____	
_____	_____	
_____	_____	
		Is your total reasonable?
_____	_____	

Total is between

_____ and _____   Total _____ _____

Use your menu to write the prices on each bill. Find the total in any way you choose, including the use of a calculator.

2.

Shooting Star Snack Shop		Customer's Name:
Item	Price(¢)	_____
Grilled Cheese	_____	
Potato Chips	_____	
Fruit Salad Cup	_____	
_____	_____	
_____	_____	Is your total reasonable?
Total is between		
_____ and _____	Total _____	_____

3.

Shooting Star Snack Shop		Customer's Name:
Item	Price(¢)	_____
Pizza Slice	_____	
Carrot Sticks	_____	
Lemonade	_____	
_____	_____	
_____	_____	Is your total reasonable?
Total is between		
_____ and _____	Total _____	_____

Snack Shop Addition

Many Ways to Solve a Problem

Solve the following problem two different ways. Use pictures and words to describe how you found the answer.

$$\begin{array}{r} 67 \\ + \underline{55} \end{array}$$

First Way:

Second Way:

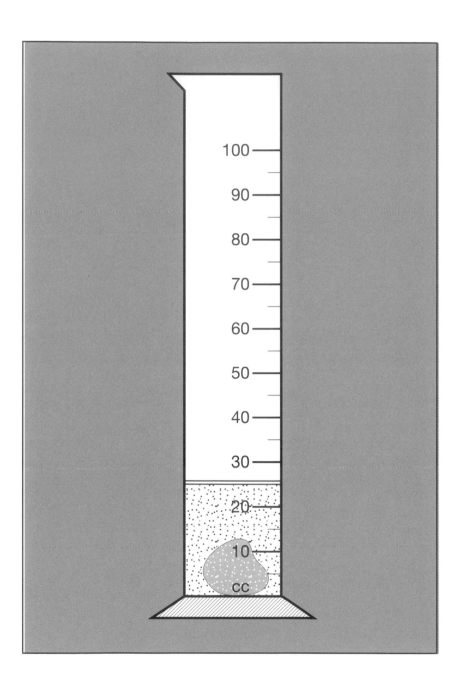

Unit 10
Exploring Volume

	Student Guide	Adventure Book	Unit Resource Guide*
Lesson 1			
Reading Scales	@		
Lesson 2			
Reading Graduated Cylinders	@		
Lesson 3			
Filling Graduated Cylinders	@		
Lesson 4			
Measuring Volume	@		
Lesson 5			
Problem Solving with Volume	@		

Unit Resource Guide pages are from the teacher materials.

Scales Worksheet 1

Look at the scale to the right.

Write the number for each letter.

A. _____

B. _____

C. _____

D. _____

E. _____

F. _____

Make an arrow at 85, and mark it "G."

Make an arrow at 97, and mark it "H."

Scales Worksheet 2

Look at the scale to the right.

Write the number for each letter.

A. _____

B. _____

C. _____

D. _____

E. _____

F. _____

Make an arrow at 110, and mark it "G."

Make an arrow at 119, and mark it "H."

F ⟶ 100

E ⟶

D ⟶

C ⟶

B ⟶ 20

A ⟶

120

80

60

40

0

Scales Worksheet 3

For problems 1 and 2, write the temperature the thermometer shows.

For problem 3, color the thermometer to show 85°. For problem 4, show 103°.

Scales Worksheet 4

For problems 1 and 2, write the speed that each speedometer shows.

1.   **2.**

_____   _____

For problems 3 and 4, draw an arrow to show the speed on each speedometer.

3.   **4.**

80 mph   55 mph

Scales at Home

Homework

Dear Family Member:

In class, we have been looking at examples of scales, such as thermometers, metersticks, and so on. Please help your child as he or she looks around your home for other examples of scales.

Thank you for your cooperation.

Look around your home for several examples of scales. Examples include control knobs for the oven, radio tuners, rulers, and so on. Draw a picture of two or three scales that you find. Include both the numbers and the units, if you can. Then, write about each scale. Tell what it is and how it is used.

Understanding Scales

Look at the scale to the right.

Write the number for each letter.

A. _____

B. _____

C. _____

D. _____

E. _____

F. _____

Make an arrow at 62, and mark it "G."

Make an arrow at 75, and mark it "H."

F ⟶ 80

70

60

50

E ⟶

D ⟶ 40

30

C ⟶

B ⟶ 20

10

A ⟶

0

Reading Graduated Cylinders

Collect

Work with a partner to read the graduated cylinders your teacher has put around the room.

Cylinder	V Volume in _____ unit		
	Partner 1	Partner 2	Agreed Reading

Scales and Meniscus

Homework

Dear Family Member:

In class, we have been reading the level of water in a graduated cylinder by paying attention to the **meniscus**—the shape of the surface of the water. We read the line at the bottom of the meniscus. You can help provide additional practice for your child by gathering various glass and plastic containers, including a measuring cup with a scale on it. If necessary, please assist your child as he or she fills these containers with water.

Thank you for your cooperation.

1. Fill some glass and plastic containers with water. Look at the water level in each container. Do you see a meniscus? Is it easier to see the meniscus in a glass container or a plastic container? Write about what happened.

A graduated cylinder containing 69 cc.

_____

_____

_____

_____

_____

2. Find a measuring cup with a scale on it. What kind of scale is on the measuring cup? Draw a picture of the scale on the measuring cup. Then, write about the scale, and explain how it is used.

Reading Graduated Cylinders

Reading a 2-Cup Measure

Homework

Look at the three pictures below. Each of the three children is trying to read the water level in the 2-cup measure. Explain the correct and incorrect methods you see.

A.   **B.**   **C.**   2 CUPS

Picture A: _____

_____

_____

Picture B: _____

_____

_____

Picture C: _____

_____

_____

Filling Graduated Cylinders

Work with a partner to fill and read water levels in graduated cylinders.

Materials

- beaker filled with water
- eyedropper
- graduated cylinder
- paper towels (to clean up spills)

The eyedropper helps you get exact volumes.

Directions

1. One partner names a target volume such as 50 cc or 75 cc.

2. The second partner pours water into the graduated cylinder to reach the target volume. Use the dropper to add a little extra water, if needed.

3. The first partner reads the volume and writes it down in the data table on the next page.

4. The second partner checks the reading and writes it down.

5. Both partners agree on the reading and record it.

6. After both partners agree, pour the water back into the beaker.

7. Repeat the process taking turns.

First Partner's Reading	Second Partner's Reading	Agreed Reading

How to Fill a Graduated Cylinder

Explain how to fill a graduated cylinder correctly. Use clue words like *first, next,* and *finally* to tell the steps in order.

_____

_____

_____

_____

_____

_____

Draw a picture showing how to fill a graduated cylinder.

Remember to show the scale.

Measuring Volume

Draw

Draw a picture of the lab setup.

Collect

Fill a graduated cylinder with 80 cc of water. Pick at least four objects, including a chain of centimeter connecting cubes. Fill in the data table.

Measuring Volume Data Table 1

Object	V (Water) in _____ unit	V (Total) in _____ unit	V (Object) in _____ unit

Graph

Make a bar graph of your data on a piece of bar graph paper.

Explore

Work together to answer the following questions.

1. Which object has the most volume? What is its volume?

_____

_____

2. Which object has the least volume? What is its volume?

_____

_____

3. What is the difference in volume between the two objects? Show how you found your answer.

_____

4. Look at Measuring Volume Data Table 1. Find the volume of three times the number of objects listed in the first column. If the water level is at 80 cc, which objects will overflow the 100 cc mark on the graduated cylinder?

Use Measuring Volume Data Table 2 to write your answers.

Measuring Volume Data Table 2

Object	V (Object) in _____ unit	V (triple) in _____ unit	Overflow 100 cc mark (Yes or No)

How Many Will It Take to Overflow?

Homework

Collect

Ask an adult for help in choosing the materials listed below:

- 1 clear container (jar or glass)
- various objects, such as marbles, coins, nuts and bolts, and so on, that will sink and fit in the container (Don't choose very small objects.)
- tape or marker
- water
- paper towels

Directions

1. Fill the container with water almost to the top.

2. Mark the level of the water with tape or a marker.

3. Estimate how many of the same type of object will make the water overflow in the container.

4. Drop the objects carefully, one at a time, into the container. How many objects did it take to make the water level overflow?

5. Record the data you gather in the chart below.

6. Refill the container with water to the marked level. Drop another type of object.

Object	Estimated Number of Objects (to make the container overflow)	Actual Number of Objects (to make the container overflow)

Volume Math Check

What is the volume of the clay in the cylinder labeled "after"?
Write a number sentence to show how you got your answer.

_____

_____

before

after

Room for Ripley

In the book *Room for Ripley,* Carlos put the castle into the bowl before he began adding the water. After the water was in the bowl he added the fish. Explain what would happen if Carlos filled the bowl to the top with water and then tried to add the castle, plants, and fish. Be sure to talk about why it would happen.

Volume Problem 1

Bill's rock has a volume of 25 cc. He put in 50 cc of water. What is the water level with both the object and the water in the graduated cylinder? Show the water level by shading the graduated cylinder with your pencil or crayon.

Explain how you got your answer.

_____

_____

_____

_____

Volume Problem 2

Marlene has two objects. One object has a volume of 15 cc. The other object has a volume of 18 cc. She placed both objects in 60 cc of water.

What will be the volume reading of the graduated cylinder? Write a number sentence to show how you got your answer.

_____

_____

Volume Problem 3

Jim put 40 cc of water in a graduated cylinder. He found the volume of Object A to be 6 cc. The volume reading with both objects in the graduated cylinder is 65 cc. Jim said, "I can figure out the volume of Object B without taking Object A out."

What is the volume of Object B? Use number sentences to help explain how you got your answer.

_____

_____

_____

_____

_____

Clayton's Volume Problem

Homework

Dear Family Member:

Your child is learning to read volumes on graduated cylinders. Help your child complete the problem below.

Thank you for your cooperation.

Clayton put 12 centimeter connecting cubes in water.
The graduated cylinder reads 72 cc.

How much water is in the graduated cylinder?
Write a number sentence to show how you got your answer.

_____

_____

_____

Glossary

This glossary provides definitions or examples of key terms in the Grade 2 lessons as a resource for students and parents. See the Glossary in the *Teacher Implementation Guide* for more detailed definitions.

A

Area (Unit 16)
The amount of space a shape covers. Area is measured in square units.

B

Base-ten Pieces (Unit 6)
A set of blocks that students use to represent numbers. A skinny is made of 10 bits and a flat is made of 100 bits.

Nickname	Picture
bit	
skinny	
flat	

Bit (Unit 6)
The smallest of the base-ten pieces. It often represents 1. (See also base-ten pieces.)

C

Centimeter (Unit 5)
A unit of length in the metric system. A centimeter (cm) is 1/100 of a meter. This rectangle is one centimeter long.

Cone (Unit 17)
A three-dimensional shape. Examples:

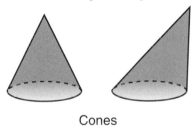

Cones

Corner (Unit 15)
A corner is the point where two sides or edges of a shape meet.

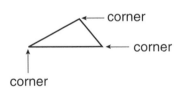

Cube (Unit 17)
A three-dimensional shape with six square faces that are all the same size.

Cube Model (Unit 7)
A shape made with connecting cubes.

Cube Model Plan (Unit 7)
A grid that shows how to build a cube model. The number in each square shows the number of cubes stacked over that square.

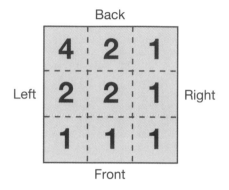

See the picture of the cube model for this plan under Cube Model.

Cubic Centimeter (Unit 10)
The volume of a cube that is one centimeter long on each edge.

cubic centimeter

Cubit (Unit 4)
A very old unit of length. It is the distance from the elbow to the tip of the longest finger.

Cylinder (Unit 15)
A three-dimensional shape. Examples:

Cylinders   Not a Cylinder

D

E

Edge (Unit 17)
A line where two faces of a three-dimensional shape meet.

edge

Equal-arm Balance (Unit 8)
A tool for measuring the mass of an object.

Estimate (Unit 4)
1. (adjective) a number that is close to the desired number
2. (verb) to approximate

Even Number (Unit 2)
Numbers that are doubles. The numbers 0, 2, 4, 6, 8, 10, . . . etc. are even. The number 28 is even because it is 14 + 14.

F

Face (Unit 17)
A two-dimensional shape that is one side of a three-dimensional shape.

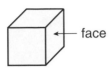
face

Fact Families (Unit 11)
Related math facts. These four number sentences are a fact family:
$1 + 2 = 3$
$2 + 1 = 3$
$3 - 2 = 1$
$3 - 1 = 2$

Flat (Unit 6)
A block that is one of the base-ten pieces. A flat is made of 100 bits. It often represents 100. (See also base-ten pieces.)

Flip (Unit 15)
A way of moving a two-dimensional shape. These dotted triangles are flipped over the lines.

or

Function Machine (Unit 19)
A "machine" that follows a rule. It gives exactly one output number for any input number. This is a data table for an "Add 2" machine.

Input	Output
0	2
1	3
5	7
18	20

G

Gram (Unit 8)
The basic unit used to measure mass in the metric system. An ounce is about 28 grams. One gram is about the mass of a raisin.

H

Hand Span (Unit 4)
The distance from the tip of your thumb to the tip of your baby finger with your hand spread as wide as possible.

Horizontal Axis (Unit 2)
In a coordinate grid, the left/right axis.

I

Interval (Unit 2 & Unit 5)
All the numbers between (and including) two numbers.

J

K

L

Leftover (Unit 12 & Unit 19)
A number that remains or is left in a problem about equal sharing.

Line Symmetry (Unit 15)
A shape has line symmetry if it can be folded into two matching halves.

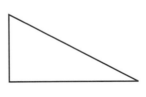

This shape has line symmetry.   This shape does not have line symmetry.

Line of Symmetry (Unit 15)
A line through a shape. If you fold the shape along this line, then one half of the figure matches the other.

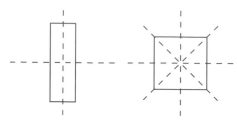

The dotted lines are lines of symmetry.

M

Mass (Unit 8 & Unit 10)
The amount of matter in an object.

Median (Unit 5)
The number "in the middle" of a set of data. Example: Jonah rolled a car down a ramp three times. The first time it rolled 30 cm. The second time it rolled 28 cm. The third time it rolled 33 cm. He put the numbers in order: 28 cm, 30 cm, 33 cm. 30 cm is the median because it is in the "middle" of his data.

Meniscus (Unit 10)
The curved surface formed when a liquid creeps up the side of a graduated cylinder.

A graduated cylinder
containing 69 cc.

Meter (Unit 5)
A unit of length in the metric system. A meter is a bit more that 39 inches.

Mr. Origin (Unit 18)
A plastic figure that helps children learn about direction and distance. Mr. Origin has a mitten on his right hand and a button on his front.

Multiplication Number Sentence (Unit 12)
A number sentence uses numbers and symbols instead of words to describe a problem. A multiplication number sentence describes a multiplication problem. For example, a multiplication number sentence for the problem "5 birds landed on a branch. Each bird had two seeds. How many seeds do all 5 birds have?" is $5 \times 2 = 10$.

N

Number Sentence (Unit 12)
A number sentence uses numbers and symbols instead of words to describe a problem. For example, a number sentence for the problem "5 birds landed on a branch. Two more birds also landed on the branch. How many birds are on the branch?" is $5 + 2 = 7$.

O

Odd Number (Unit 2)
A number that is not even. The odd numbers are 1, 3, 5, 7, 9, and so on.

P

Parallel Lines (Unit 15)
Lines that do not meet. Lines that are always the same distance apart.

Perimeter (Unit 20)
The distance around a two-dimensional shape.

Place Value (Unit 6)
The value of a digit in a number. For example, the 5 is in the hundreds place in 4573, so it stands for 500.

Prism (Unit 17)
A 3-dimensional shape. Examples:

Prisms   Not a prism

Pyramid (Unit 17)
A 3-dimensional shape. Examples.

Triangular pyramid   Rectangular pyramid

Q

R

Rectangle (Unit 15)
A shape with four sides and with four square corners.

Rectangles   Not a rectangle

Rectangular Prism (Unit 17)
A prism whose faces are all rectangles.

Rectangular prism

Rectangular Pyramid (Unit 17)
A pyramid with a rectangle for a base.

Rectangular pyramid

Reflection (Unit 15)
See flip.

Related Facts (Unit 11)
Fact families. For example, these facts are related:
$1 + 2 = 3$
$2 + 1 = 3$
$3 - 2 = 1$
$3 - 1 = 2$

Remainder (Unit 12)
A number that remains or is left after a division problem.

Rotation (Unit 15)
See turn.

Rotational Symmetry (Unit 15)
See turn symmetry.

S

Sample (Unit 13)
A smaller group taken out of a large collection.

Skinny (Unit 6)
A block that is one of the base-ten pieces. It is made of 10 bits. It often represents 10. (See also base-ten pieces.)

Slide (Unit 15)
A way of moving a two-dimensional shape. It moves a shape a certain distance in a certain direction.

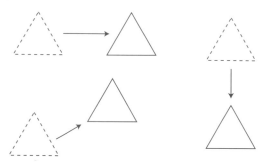

Sliding a triangle

Sphere (Unit 17)
A three-dimensional shape. A basketball is a common object shaped like a sphere.

Square (Unit 4 & Unit 15)
A rectangle that has four sides of equal length.

Squares   Not a
                 Square

Square Centimeter (sq cm) (Unit 16)
The area of a square that is 1 cm long on each side.

1 square centimeter

Standard Unit of Measure (Unit 5)
Universally accepted quantities used in measuring variables, e.g., centimeters and inches are standard units used to measure length and square centimeters and square inches are used to measure area.

Sum (Unit 3)
The answer to an addition problem.

Survey (Unit 19)
An investigation carried out by collecting data and then analyzing it.

T

Tally Marks (Unit 2)
A way to record a count by making marks. Tallies are usually grouped in fives, 卌 |||.

Translation (Unit 15)
See slide.

Trapezoid (Unit 15)
A four-sided shape with exactly one pair of parallel sides.

Trapezoids   Not Trapezoids

Triangular Prism (Unit 17)
A prism with a triangular base.

Triangular prisms

Triangular Pyramid (Unit 17)
A pyramid with a triangular base.

Triangular pyramid

Turn (Unit 15)
A way of moving a two-dimensional shape. A turn moves a shape around a point in its center.

Before   After
Triangle before and after half turn.

Turn Symmetry (Unit 15)

A shape has turn symmetry if you can turn it around a point in its center so that it "fits" itself. For example, a square has turn symmetry.

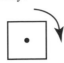

Two-dimensional Shapes (Unit 17)

Flat shapes.

U

Unit (of Measurement) (Unit 10 & Unit 16)

A fixed amount used to measure. For example, centimeter, foot, kilogram, and quart are units of measurement.

V

Value (Unit 13)

The possible outcomes of a variable. For example, red, green, and blue are possible values for the variable *color*. Two meters and 6 inches are possible values for the variable *length*.

Variable (Unit 4 & Unit 13)

Something that changes or varies in an investigation.

Vertex (Unit 17)

See corner.

Volume (Unit 6, Unit 7 & Unit 10)

The measure of the amount of space occupied by an object. Volume is measured in cubic units.

W

Width (of a rectangle) (Unit 16)

The distance along one side of a rectangle is the length and the distance along an adjacent side is the width.

X

Y

Z

Index

The index provides page references for the *Student Guide*. Definition or explanation of key terms can be found in the glossary. A good source for information on the location of topics in the curriculum is the *Scope and Sequence* in Section 5 of the *Teacher Implementation Guide*.

Edge, 507
Estimation
addition, 217–218, 229, 237–240, 243–244
counting, 67
length, 55, 85–91, 107–114, 119–120
measurement, 94
subtraction, 293, 295

Face, shapes, 507, 509
Fractions, 365–375, 379–415, 577, 581–592
addition, 379–383
and area, 459–461
area model, 379–391, 415
paper folding and, 367–373
Function machine, 555–563, 579–580
Functions, 555–571

Games
Add to 100, 232
Cover Up Game, 43
Difference War, 299
Fraction Concentration, 413–414
Fraction War, 413–414
Monkey Treats, 323–325
Moving on the 200 Chart, 27–29
Not More Than 100, 139
Take Your Places, Please, 151–155
Spin and Add, 31–33
Geoboard, 589
area on, 479–486
puzzles, 483–486
Geometry riddles, 511
Graduated cylinder, reading volume, 236–281
Grouping and counting, 55, 65, 67, 83
Grouping and sharing, 313–314

Half-inch grid paper, 313–314
Halves, 441
Height, 70–74, 81–85
measurement, 106
Hemisphere, 515

Input-output data table, 555–556, 563, 579–580
Interval, 94

King Gupta, 227

Labs
Classifying and Sorting Lids, 344–345
Colors of Shoes at My Home, 75–77
Counting Kids, 547–550
High, Wide, and Handsome, 70–74
Marshmallows and Containers, 157
Measuring Mass, 205–209
Measuring Volume, 267–270
Mr. Origin Left/Right or Front/Back, 535–538
Rolling along in Centimeters, 113–117
Undercover Investigation, 357–358
Length
estimation, 55, 107–114, 119–120
measurement, 70–74, 81–91, 94, 103–117
of a rectangle, 467, 471

Tallies, 83
Ten frames, 13–18
    empty, 11
Tile designs, 20–23
Time, telling to the nearest 5 minutes, 125–130
Transformations, 425–437, 444–450
    flips, 427, 443, 450
    slides, 423–425
    turns, 426
Triangle Flash Cards
    Group A, 59–61
        Group A Subtraction, 285–286
    Group B, 79–80
        Group B Subtraction, 315–316
    Group C, 95–96
        Group C Subtraction, 349–350
    Group D, 131–132
        Group D Subtraction, 377–378
    Group E, 169–170
        Group E Subtraction, 419–420
    Group F, 201–202
        Group F Subtraction, 457–458
    Group G, 219–220
        Group G Subtraction, 497–498
Triangular prism, 488, 507, 509, 515
Triangular pyramid, 488, 507, 515

Variables, 113
Vertex, of shapes, 507, 509
Volume, 179, 183–184, 187–191
    of containers, 157–163
    of cubes, 172–176
    in cubic centimeters, 259, 263–270, 273, 277–281

Width, of a rectangle, 467, 471
Word problems, 4–9, 39–41, 63, 161–163, 218,
        221–222, 235, 301, 321, 324–330, 334–336,
        339–340, 585–586. *See also* TIMS Laboratory
        experiments